PR(HAVE BEEN A
NEW YORK CITY
TRANSIT COP

Tim,

It was great to see you again. I always enjoy your company and am delighted to hear about the wonderful life you and Colleen have made for yourselves and your family. I can't believe you guys are already sending a child off to college — where has the time gone?

It was nice to hear you talk about my dad. Like your father, he touched the many people he came into contact with in a special way. When you read his book, I think you will feel like he is sitting right next to you, telling you some of his many stories! I know he would be proud of the man you have become and what you have accomplished.

Enjoy the book!

PROUD TO HAVE BEEN A NEW YORK CITY TRANSIT COP

JOHN R. MARTIN

Outskirts Press, Inc.
Denver, Colorado

Outskirts Press, Inc.
http://www.outskirtspress.com

ISBN: 978-1-4327-6589-7

Outskirts Press and the "OP" logo are trademarks belonging to Outskirts Press, Inc.

PRINTED IN THE UNITED STATES OF AMERICA

Foreword

With all the books and TV shows out there, another cop story? Right, but this one's really different. It's not only a story about police work and policemen; it's a story about all kinds of people. It's a story about two native New Yorkers who joined the New York City Transit Police Department after service in the Armed Forces during World War II. It's a story about how these two guys helped to make the Transit Police Force one of the finest, and one of the biggest, in the country. It's a story about how these two guys charmed the mayor of the City of New York, upset at least two city police commissioners, and forced the City of New York to provide improved police protection for the riding and general public. And finally, it's a study in human relations and what it takes to provide effective leadership.

John R. Martin
Captain (*Retired*), New York City Transit Police
Palm Coast, Florida
March 1995

Chapter 1

I was born in Harlem, a section of the Borough of Manhattan, New York City on January 28, 1923. I was the youngest of four children born to Gertrude and Matthew Martin. Matthew Martin died at the age of twenty-six due to the popular belief at the time in exposing everyone to a family illness. In this instance, it was scarlet fever! Mrs. Martin and the kids survived; Mr. Martin did not. He was waked at home during Christmas, since no Mass could be said on that day.

After the funeral, Gertrude Martin (her friends called her Gert) moved her brood to a cold-water flat on West 124th street, right next door to a firehouse – Hook & Ladder #40. Gert got a job at Blumstein's Department Store and proceeded with the task of raising her four children (Vivian, Matthew, Dorothy, and me). The task certainly was not easy on a salary of $18 per week (a six-day work week in those days) and Social Security had not yet arrived. Gert did her best. There was always food on the table, warm clothing for all, and everyone was in good health. Before leaving for work each morning, she had to get the three older children off to school before leaving me with her sister-in-law, our Aunt May. Aunt May was a kind, refined person who dearly loved me – I reminded her so much of her deceased brother, Matthew, my father. She had no children of her own so there was no conflict of interest, so to speak. But she was a stickler on manners and insisted that every answer include the word "ma'am." It was "Yes, ma'am; no ma'am; thank you, ma'am." When the doorbell rang at 6:30 every evening, I would rush to the door to meet my weary mother, returning from Blumstein's Department Store. I was delighted to be going home and away from all those ma'ams – still, I recognized that my aunt had many wonderful qualities and I loved her very much.

Every Easter, Aunt May bought new suits for the boys and new dresses for the girls, plus new shoes for all! In return, it was expected that the Martin family visit her apartment every Sunday and every holiday. Each child was required to do a little number – recite a poem, sing a song, tell a story, or just show up. Vivian was the most talented of the group (she later became a John Powers model, a cover girl, and an actress – she appeared onstage with Fred Stone). The rest of us had no talent, but we did the best we could. In return for our performances, we were rewarded with goodies like Seeley's Golden Ginger Ale and Horn and Hardart's cupcakes. Uncle Mac and our Grandfather, Daniel Martin, were always present and loudly applauded our efforts.

The family lifestyle continued in this fashion for about a

year, with Gert working long hours at Blumstein's, the older children in school, and me getting through my daily ritual of ma'ams. Suddenly, one day, Gert gathered her clan together to announce that we had a new Daddy! She had just married Peter McMahon, a widowed fireman who already had five children of his own. I guess that's what happens when you live next door to a firehouse!

New quarters were a must for this new family of nine, so a five-room apartment was found on 127th Street and Convent Avenue. It was a nice apartment, complete with a new refrigerator, over which a huge shelf was located. This shelf became the favorite refuge for both my new brother Tommy and me. Too often, Tommy and I had to flee our parents' wrath for some devilish act we committed while acting in concert! Poor Tommy (only nine months older than me) always bore the brunt of everything, not only for what he and I did together, but he had to take the rap for whatever rash acts of his brothers and sisters. For you see, it was not easy for our new father (we called him "Dada Pete") to administer justice after returning home from his fire duties to his recently combined brood. There were always reports of "Peter did this, Winnie did that, Vincent did this, and Tommy and Jack did something else." I'm sure poor Dada Pete wanted to dispense even-handed justice to all the kids. But psychologically, he was restrained by the knowledge that he had not fathered all of them. Unlike in the fairytale Cinderella, he was much tougher on his own kids than he was on his stepchildren. I know my stepbrothers and stepsisters saw this as grossly unfair. Nonetheless, Dada Pete was a fine man, a hard worker, and a good provider – all on a weekly salary of $60. That was very good money during the depression, even with nine kids. He was a big man, over six feet tall with broad shoulders, plenty of muscle, and a full head of red hair. All his sons (he eventually fathered a total of six) grew to six feet or more. Even my oldest full brother, Matthew Martin, known in the neighborhood as "Big Pep," was over six feet tall. The only short one was me. Known as "Little Pep," I barely attained the height of five feet eight and a half inches – just enough to become a cop!

I really don't know how Dada Pete and Gert found enough privacy to manage having seven children of their own, but they did! Patricia, Robert, Jean, Donald, Bernadette, Adrianne, and Russell came along in rapid succession. And with each new addition to the family, larger living quarters were required, resulting in a continuing series of apartment moves – sometimes as many as three a year! All of us older kids (I was no longer the baby) became very proficient in the art of moving. Crates and boxes were obtained from the local grocer, where we had a running charge account. Dishes, shoes, sneakers, underwear, books, etc. were placed in these containers and the group carried them in parade-like fashion to the new apartment. Larger items such as chairs, bed springs, mattresses, and tables were carted by the older boys, leaving only a few of the very heavy items to be carted by a hired -- or borrowed -- truck. There were always looks of disbelief, dismay, and panic on the faces of our new neighbors as they tried counting the new tenants entering the premises! I'm certain they were sure that the noise level and the local ecological balance would never be the same. A bonus of these frequent moves was a freshly painted apartment, with a free month's rent!

The birth of Dada Pete's and Gert's last child, Russell, rounded the family off at fifteen (Dada Pete's oldest daughter from his first marriage lived with another relative). Now that the family size had "stabilized," frequent moves were no longer required just to accommodate the additional children. Moves took place to gain a little more creature comforts and status, such as apartments with elevators or inside bathrooms. We made one such move to the most fashionable apartment building in the neighborhood -- a stately building complete with a sidewalk canopy, elevator, house phones, a huge foyer, and two separate entrances. Located on 129th Street and Convent Avenue, this became the apple of my mother's eye. But there was a hitch. There was a strict requirement of no more than four children per family! My mother came up with a solution -- eleven of us would have to enter and leave the premises incognito!

Dada Pete and Gert rented the apartment and we were given specific assignments by our parents for entering and leaving the apartment. We quickly assumed other names such as "Cousin John" or "Cousin Winnie" so that, if asked, we could say that we were just visiting our cousins for the day. For nearly a year, we escaped full detection in spite of the fact that most of us were running amok in the hallways, or using the house phones, or wearing out the elevator. And that is to say nothing about lounging around the lobby on cold and rainy days. I do recall that the apartment had seven huge rooms with two bathrooms, plus a grand hallway as long as a bowling alley – ideal for forty-yard sprints! The apartment manager was a very dapper gentleman, usually attired in a Chesterfield coat, topped off with a black homburg hat. His normally calm demeanor was shattered many times, having to chase and then interrogate the "visiting cousins." We completely frustrated his investigative efforts, never admitting that there were actually more than four children in the family!

However, in spite of our best efforts at keeping the family secret, we were forced to move after just about a year of elegant living. We moved all the way up to the Pelham Bay section of the Bronx, where Dada Pete and Gert decided to rent a house. This was really great for the younger kids, but very rough on the older ones. For us older kids, we had become accustomed to city living and were too involved with the old neighborhood. We were not interested in making new friends, nor did we want to settle for the quiet life of suburbia. My older sisters, Vivian and Dorothy, had been working since the tender age of twelve and Big Pep from the age of eleven, to help support the rest of us. They had to travel a long way to get to work -- over an hour and a half one-way! Vivian was a model at the time; Dorothy worked at Grant's in the record section; and Big Pep was working for Jack Frost Sugar in New Jersey. Thanks to Dottie, we had all the latest records from Glenn Miller, T&J Dorsey, Benny Goodman, Harry James, Charlie Bennett, and others. But for Big Pep, he gave up his chance to play big league baseball with either the Yankees or the Giants. He was a terrific pitcher who could also hit the long ball. He gave up trying out because the family needed his sure salary as a longshoreman, rather than taking the risk on a future big league payoff. I'm sure my brother would have made it in professional baseball. When he was trying out for the Yankees, Bill Dickey, the famous catcher for the Yankees, drove my brother home one night. What a thrill that was!

In any event, the trip was murder for the older kids. So, after about one year, the family moved back to the old neighborhood. This time we landed on 125th Street and St. Nicholas Avenue – right around the corner from the firehouse. Happy days were here again! One cold winter night, Dada Pete developed pneumonia while fighting a big fire in Harlem. Never one for a hospital or extended bed care, he left his sickbed, got dressed, and walked to the firehouse to pick up his pay. While climbing the two flights of stairs upon his return to the new apartment, he suffered a heart attack. He would never return to the fire duty he loved. He was placed on extended sick leave and after one year, he was forced to retire, without a pension. In those days, they had no disability pensions. The family returned to the Pelham Bay area again, this time buying a house on the same street they lived on earlier. Back in 1938, you could buy a house for $4,500 with a down payment of $500. This time around, none of us really complained given Dada Pete's rapidly failing health. He lingered for another year, finally succumbing in October 1939. He was a great guy, a good father, a fine husband, and a dedicated fireman. He had to make it to heaven – he sure worked hard for all of us.

Poor Gert once again faced life as a widow – only now she had fifteen kids to worry about, not just four. She was no longer twenty-four years old as she had been when my father passed away, and she felt as if no man could replace Dada Pete. I don't know how she managed, but she did. My brother Tommy and I, both fifteen at the time, became the official family chauffeurs. The fact that you were required to be eighteen to legally drive a car was a minor inconvenience. We drove hoping we would not be stopped and asked to produce a valid driver's license. Tommy was big and strong and easily passed for eighteen. Me, I took to smoking cigars and wearing fedoras to get by. On the few occasions that we did get stopped by the cops and asked to produce our license, we managed to talk the officers out of arresting us by telling them our tales of woe. "Officer, Dad was a deceased fireman who left a widow and fifteen children. We were just driving to the store to get some milk for the smaller kids." Sometimes the trip was to get medicine for a sick kid. Whatever reason we chose, they were always sympathetic and let us go. We became expert drivers in no time. Due to a nervous condition that was the result of a freak elevator mishap years earlier, Mom was not comfortable riding on subways or other forms of public transportation. But she loved riding in the car and enjoyed driving just about anywhere. However, she didn't have much money for things like gas, oil, batteries, or tires. She thought that three gallons of gas (at thirteen cents a gallon, in those days) should last all week, and batteries and tires should last forever! Tommy and I did the best we could under the circumstances. We managed to obtain used tires and batteries when needed. Our incentive was a strong one – use of the car for ourselves a couple of nights a week. We were the envy of all our friends. They shared our car rides for the price of a gallon of gas! It sure was fun for us, and we both enjoy driving to this very day.

A few years passed and suddenly, America was bombed into World War II, on the very day that my sister Dorothy was getting married. I was driving some of the guests from the old neighborhood to the wedding in the Bronx when I met a high school chum who announced, "Hey, Pep – the Japs just bombed Pearl Harbor."

"Where the hell is that?" I asked.

He said, "I don't know, but I guess it means war."

It sure did – two days later I went down to the Federal Building to enlist in the Marines. I passed the physical and was given consent papers for Mom to sign, since I was only eighteen at the time. She refused to sign the papers! She agreed to sign the necessary papers if I enlisted in the Navy rather than the Marines -- Dada Pete had been in the Navy in World War I. My brother and pal, Tommy, had already enlisted in the Navy that past year. Since there was no changing Mom's mind, I enlisted in the Navy the next day. I settled back and waited to be called.

One of my biggest regrets at the time was that my enlistment meant the end of my basketball days. Basketball was my favorite sport and I played a lot of it. I was on the team at Rice High School and I also played for Corpus Christi Church as well as two neighborhood teams, the Senators and the Ramblers. From the time I was thirteen years old, I played basketball just about every day. I had a boyhood buddy and schoolmate named Lou Smeelings (also known as "the Blue Baron") who came to this country from Germany at the age of six. Lou and I developed the same passion for basketball and both of us played on several of the same teams, including the team at Rice High School. The wonderful times we had have never been forgotten. Lou's dad, Herman, was in the German Army during World War I and he used to share his accounts of the war with us both, recalling the many horrors he saw. Lou was an only child at the time, so his parents never objected to his having me over for dinner, for lunch, even for breakfast! In fact, they seemed to enjoy the extra company. Lou's mother was a lovely lady with a terrific sense of humor. Herman was a really comical guy who was always ready to tell us stories. We loved it! When World War II started, Lou's dad begged me not to go. "War is horrible – nobody wins really," he said.

"This war is different, Mr. Smeelings," I said, "they dealt us a sneak punch and the Germans are on their side. I've got to go. I want to go." And so I went, reporting to the Federal

Building at 90 Church Street on a Sunday morning. I was wearing my Rambler basketball jacket, slacks, and saddle shoes. I was shipped by train to the Naval Training Station at Newport, Rhode Island along with about 500 other guys. For the first time in my eighteen years on this planet, I was on my own. Well, to the extent that someone serving in the US Navy can be considered on his own!

Naval recruit training (boot camp) was stepped up during war time, reduced from twelve weeks to just six weeks. As a result, some of the finer points of seamanship were glossed over. About the only seaman's knots most of us sailors learned were a square knot and a bowline. No matter, we would learn the others elsewhere. Boot camp flew by and after one month, we all lined up happily for our first payday. I was paid a sum of $21 and minus the cost of incidentals – haircuts, uniform tailoring, etc. – I wound up with a hot $9 net pay! But money didn't matter much, since at the time, we recruits got only limited liberty. A USO dance at the "Y" was pretty much it. At the end of six weeks, we graduated from the Naval Training Station and were given our new assignments. I was assigned to a new destroyer being outfitted in the Brooklyn Navy Yard, *the USS Bailey* (DD 492). About fifty of us recruits from Newport were shipped by train to New York where we were taken to the Receiving station located at 52nd Street and the Hudson River. Here we spent a hectic two days before being shipped to the *Bailey*.

I was to spend the next four years aboard her, and what

an exciting four years it was! Going from the frozen waste-
lands and freezing waters of the Aleutians to the torrid heat
of Borneo, there was plenty of action to speak about. The
Bailey earned nine Battle Stars plus a Navy Unit Citation.
She was a fine ship and my years aboard her, and the experiences I had, have never left me. It was, in a way, my college
campus. A framed, official photograph of the *Bailey* is in
my study (my finished basement, really) and many a night,
I sit in my easy chair, look at that picture, and think back
to those action-filled and fun-packed days. Usually in the
middle of some vivid recollection of a particularly wild liberty, with background music supplied by a Big Band record,
the phone will ring or my wife will remind me to take out
the garbage. Suddenly, I am jerked back to the present! But
just for a little while, I am a young sailor again and life isn't
so complicated. One final note on my naval career -- I ended up a Quartermaster 2nd Class and probably would have
remained in the Navy had I not developed an ulcer. This
was to the dismay of my brother-in-law, Captain Sydney
Bunting, USN, who had married my sister, Vivian, just before the war started. Even someone of Captain Bunting's
stature could not change the Navy medical standards – an
ulcer was cause for a medical discharge. I was honorably
discharged from the US Navy on February 21st, 1946.

For the next few months, I spent my time renew-
ing old friendships and exchanging war stories, usually at
Naughton's Bar! And courtesy of Uncle Sam, I collected a
few "52-20" checks to keep me going. I had one suit made

of covet cloth with slightly pegged pants which I had just retrieved from Kelley's Pawn Shop upon my discharge from the Navy. After four years, the suit was still in great shape and looked a lot better than the suits that were for sale at that time. Clothing stores were trying to unload all the old suits they had on the racks. They seemed to have only two colors available, brown and blue. In fact, the salesmen didn't even bother to try to sell you. Take it or leave it! So I was very happy with my pre-war, covet cloth, olive drab suit. I was ready to go looking for a job and to dazzle the commercial world.

But I found out in a hurry that I was ill-equipped to dazzle anybody. After all, I was trained to read Morse code on a signal light; knew the Inland and International Rules of the Road; knew how to render honors to passing ships, correct navigational charts, take a star-fix, tie a bowline, wash my clothes, keep the ship's log, and take the helm. What else could I do? I couldn't even type. My brother, Tommy, had gotten out of the Navy before me and was driving a bus for the New York City Omnibus Company. Tom's run was on the 86th Street cross town in Yorkville. It ran across town from York Avenue to West End Avenue and was heavily traveled. Tom suggested that I take a few rides with him on his run to see what the life of a bus driver was like. What the heck? I wasn't working anyway and I wasn't getting anywhere fast with my job search. So, a few nights later, me and my old buddy from Rice High School, Lou Smeelings, rode my brother's bus. After a few runs across town, Tom decided to let me take the wheel! Tom figured he had taught me how to drive a car when we were both fifteen, and since the bus was only a bit bigger and I was now twenty-three, this should be a snap. The fact that the bus belonged to the bus company and carried about eighty passengers didn't enter our minds. Under Tom's watchful eye while giving rapid-fire directions, I made several successful trips and Tom pronounced me qualified! A few days later, he got hold of a job application for me, vouched for my good character, and a few days later, I got the job.

That was a big break given that I was getting married shortly to a lovely young lass from Washington Heights named Eileen Keena. The bus driver's job paid well -- about $75 per week plus overtime. The bad news – it included nights and Sundays. I was a good bus driver, but not a good employee. I hated to work on weekends. Many times I would call in sick on those Sundays I was scheduled to work and that didn't exactly make a big hit with the Irish bosses. You didn't get paid if you didn't work, so I wasn't beating the company out of my salary by not working on Sundays. It did, however, result in smaller and smaller pay checks. And naturally, this did not go over well with my new wife. Fortunately for us, her parents had left an old house to her and her brother, Jack. We had the upstairs apartment and we didn't have to worry about receiving an eviction notice if we didn't make the rent payment exactly on time. With my increasing lack of interest in driving a bus, together with the ever smaller paychecks, it became more and more difficult to make ends meet.

Eileen stood by me and encouraged me to seek a career in civil service, maybe as a fireman or policeman. I liked the idea and felt I would be good at that. I enrolled in Delehanty's Institute and started studying for the upcoming police examinations. During those times, Eileen and I were very happy with our little three-room apartment. We painted, decorated, and furnished it very nicely thanks to Eileen. My taste left something to be desired, being a fan of blue glass-covered end tables! We decorated one of the rooms with Mickey Mouse wallpaper and made this the nursery room as Eileen was expecting our first child at the time. With a baby on the way, I became a little better worker and began to earn a bit more money -- but still not as much as I could have since I was still taking the occasional Sunday off. I guess I was strictly a "Ralph Kramden" kind of bus driver.

Sometime during 1948, I met one of the guys from the old neighborhood in Naughton's bar, one night after work. He mentioned that an examination was coming up for the transit police. "The transit police – what's that?" I asked. My friend informed me that the transit police were assigned to police the city's subways. They carried guns, wore similar uniforms, had similar authority, and were paid almost as much as the city police. This all sounded pretty good to me. So, the next day, I enrolled in the course and started cramming for the forthcoming test. I went to Delehanty's about four times a week to get training in both the physical and mental aspects of the exam. By going to Delehanty's that frequently, it actually made driving a bus a lot easier. I began to hope that I would soon be some kind of a cop – city or transit – it didn't matter. I'd dream of becoming a cop and how I would look in my new uniform. I vowed to be a good officer and work my Sundays without complaining. I had no idea at the time just how difficult it would be to become a transit cop. Over 40,000 people took the examination and only about 4,000 made the list for appointment to the transit police, the Corrections Department, or The Bridge and Tunnel Authority. Making the list was no guarantee that you would get the job with the Transit Police Department – you had to be at the top of the list to even be considered for that position. And that was the job I wanted! Despite the odds, I felt confident that someday I would be appointed to the Force.

Chapter 2

Our luck was holding up, with Eileen having only recently given birth to a beautiful little girl we named Susan Eileen. Poor Eileen had a terrible breech birth delivery. Her scars and injuries from that birth are still with her to this day. She always maintained that Susan was certainly worth all the pain and discomfort she suffered. The baby brought us even closer together and our days and nights were filled with happiness. We took the baby everywhere we could. Eileen always had Susan dressed in such pretty outfits. People would stop us on the streets, in the subways, or on the bus – just to talk to the child and comment on her looks and her outfits. I now had two beautiful girls to show off. What uncomplicated and happy days those were! Not much money, but plenty of happiness. All of this before TV, with just the radio offering plenty of good music and interesting programs.

Since we lived in my wife's house, I had some chores to perform for which I was ill-prepared. They included collecting the rent from our two tenants; taking care of the coal burning furnace, including removing the ashes; and making various and sundry minor repairs. As an example of my proficiency at doing chores, during the terrible blizzard of 1947, I neglected to put out the ashes for several days. I simply let the ashes pile up in the basement. The snow was so high on the streets that the sanitation department could not get through to pick up the refuse. I was forced into desperate action when the pile of ashes started to block the doorway to the cellar stairs. I enlisted the support of my brother-in-law, Jack Keena, to help me remove roughly eight huge barrels of ashes from the basement. We put the barrels on a borrowed dolly and wheeled them to a vacant lot alongside the post office, fleeing the scene as quickly as possible once we made our deposit! I was equally inept at making repairs around the house. So it was something of a relief when we sold the house, paid off our debts, and had about $700 left. We really felt solvent with that huge sum of money! Just prior to selling the house, I was called by the Civil Service Commission and offered a position as a court officer in the city's Magistrates Courts, having been selected based on my position on the transit police list. It was explained to me that the acceptance of the court officer position would not remove my name from the transit police list and if I accepted the court officer position, I could then decide at the time transit police appointments were being made to either become a transit cop, or remain a court officer. A perfect option for a disgruntled bus driver! I accepted the court officer position and was sworn in along with about twenty-five others in the Chief Magistrate's Office at 100 Centre Street.

I was assigned to the Bronx Magistrates Court located at 161st Street and 3rd Avenue and reported there directly after being sworn in downtown. No formal training program was in existence at that time and I was given a briefing by a senior court officer who was going on vacation the next day. Understandably, he was in a hurry to get away early that day so he could begin his vacation. In substance, his instructions were as follows: "Get yourself a blue police shirt and pants; put your court officer's shield on the shirt; and report to the Court Clerk at 8 tomorrow morning. The first thing you do in the morning is obtain the court papers [affidavits] which contain the official charges. Stamp the docket numbers on them and enter the numbers in the docket book. Then go into the court room and call the names of the people present. Inform them of the charges and determine how they intend to plead to those charges, if they are represented by counsel, and so forth. Line up the ones who are pleading guilty so that you can get those cases out of the way before the other court business begins – hearings, trials, and arraignments. Then wait in the corridor for the judge to arrive and escort him to his chambers, briefing him on the court calendar. Next, lead the judge into the courtroom and announce, 'Order in the court – please rise – his honor, the judge of this court – be seated.' Then call the summons cases, inform the defendants of the charges, advise them of their rights, and obtain their pleas. At this point, the judge will render his decisions and levy the fines, sentences, and dismissals. Further, when the business of the court is finished, take the court papers back to the clerk's office and enter the dispositions in the docket book. Also, prepare the court summonses and bench warrants."

By then it was quitting time and my court officer instructor impatiently asked if I had any questions. Sensing his mood and his desire to get his vacation started, I didn't ask a thing. Nor did I let him know I was terrified! I had never even been in a courthouse before that day and the thought of helping to run one put me in a state of shock. Despite my fears and apprehensions, I thanked him for his help, wished him a good vacation, and dashed off to buy the police shirt and pants. I went straight home to tell Eileen all about the new job and begged her to pray for me. I reported to my new boss early the next morning in my uniform, proudly displaying shield #377 of the city's Magistrates Courts on my uniform shirt. I did my necessary pre-court paperwork, and after obtaining a description of the presiding judge, awaited his arrival in the corridor. The judge had been described as a "Sidney Greenstreet" type -- complete with a big wide white hat and huge cigar. A few minutes later, the judge made his entrance. I couldn't miss him! He beamed when I shouted, "Good morning, Your Honor." It was like making points with an Admiral!

"Good morning, Officer," he replied. "Come into my chambers." Suddenly, there I was, an Officer of the Court, talking to the Judge of the Court in his own chambers. I introduced myself and then proceeded to answer his questions about myself. "How long have you been an officer? Were you in the service? Where did you go to school?" The judge was very nice and really put me at ease. We discussed the court calendar and before you knew it, I was ready for my court debut.

I led the judge into the court, announced his presence, got everyone seated and obtained order. I then called the first case. I froze as I looked at the name – Norman Lipshits! I hoped no one would laugh at the pronunciation of the gentleman's name, or laugh at me. Fortunately for us both, no one did. I guess they didn't dare with a Judge Sidney Greenstreet-type presiding. After that, it was duck soup and at the end of the day, I felt like I had been a court officer for years. I knew I would love the job and it was a great opportunity to learn many facets of the criminal justice system. The hours were ideal, all day work, with Saturdays, Sundays and all holidays off. For the first time since our marriage, I had a job with normal hours. We took full advantage of my off-duty time, catching up on seeing people and going places we couldn't before. We bought a used car, a 1940 Dodge that turned out to be some bomb. It always seemed to stall out every time we went over the Whitestone Bridge on the way to the beach or house hunting on Long Island. Still, it managed to take us many places including Annapolis, Maryland where we visited my sister, Vivian, my brother-in-law, retired Navy Captain Syd Bunting, and my nephew, Geoffrey. It was hard to get a bargain on a used car in those days!

After about nine months' tenure as a court officer, I received a telegram from the Civil Service Commission directing me to report to the Transit Police Department for appointment as a patrolman. The telegram arrived just before Christmas 1949 and directed me to report for a physical on January 3, 1950. Eileen and I were on the horns of a dilemma since there was little time to consider the job change. She loved the work hours I enjoyed as a court officer and realized as a cop, I would be working around-the-clock with rotating days off. Our whole lifestyle would change dramatically and a salary increase of $300 per year seemed small compensation for what I would give up. My co-workers in the court advised me to stay in the court system where the work environment was so much better than policing the city's subways. But, deep down inside, I really wanted to be a police officer. I ignored everyone's advice, most notably my wife's, and reported for my physical as ordered.

About 300 guys were there for their physicals that morning, coming in all shapes and sizes. I noticed two other court officers there – both named Murphy. One was kind of quiet, and the other was a one-man show! He entertained us and got us relaxed enough to get through our medical examinations. It was like World War II all over again! And since we were all veterans, it was easy to organize us and direct us through our paces. After stripping down, bending over, reading eye charts, lifting weights, taking blood pressure readings, submitting to hearing tests, etc., we were told to get dressed and ushered into a large hall. Six sergeants were seated at a long table on which rested some 300 police shields, procedure manuals, and some instruction sheets. The sergeants were assisted by six patrolmen and soon we were being called to attention. Our first roll call was conducted by one of the sergeants and he instructed us to come forward as our names were called to receive our shields, manuals, and instruction sheets. As each man returned to his spot, the other guys would ask "What number did you get?" You heard loud groans if a guy got a two-digit number, like eleven or thirteen. My luck was still holding out – I got a three-digit number – and believe it or not, the number was 666. At the time, I was unaware of all the Biblical interpretation being attributed to my new shield number. I just knew the number was unique and I was happy to have it.

We were sworn in after we received our shields and had to fork over ten cents – a nickel to cover the Oath of Office and a nickel for the safety pin for our shield. We were then directed to purchase our service revolvers (Smith-Wesson or Colt .38 caliber), order our recruit training uniforms, our regulation police uniforms, nightsticks, flashlights, notebooks, and other miscellaneous items. A list of approved police equipment dealers was distributed with no specific recommendations made – a fair practice for both the dealers and the recruits. Before being dismissed, we were assigned in groups of fifty to classes designated A-B-C-D-E-F. Those ranging in height from five foot ten to six foot six were assigned to classes D-E-F. Those between five foot eight and five foot ten were assigned to classes A-B-C. I was assigned to class B. After receiving our class assignments, we all dashed off in groups to purchase our equipment, exchanging names and agreeing on which dealer to visit first.

I was fortunate in that two of the guys in my class were from the old neighborhood. Imagine the odds of that! Eight million people in this town, 40,000 guys take the police test, 4,000 wind up on the list, and 3 of us from the old neighborhood land in the same academy class! The three of us headed for the uniform firm of Smith-Grey because we heard they made the best uniforms. We knew they cost more, but we felt the extra cost was worth it. The information proved true about their uniforms lasting longer, at least in my case. I still have my original uniform coats plus a pair of the original pants – after 29 ½ years of use! After being measured for our uniforms by the tailor, we signed the credit notes to cover the cost, and were off to the city police equipment bureau to purchase our green cotton recruit training uniforms, nightsticks, and leather goods. The next stop was the gunsmith to purchase our service revolvers. Again, we signed the credit notes to cover the gun purchases (the guy threw in free carrying cases for our shields!). The cost of all this equipment was about $500, and since not too many of us recruits had that kind of cash laying around, we started the new job plunged heavily into debt. But we felt it would be worth it in the long run. Look at the benefits – a steady job, sick leave coverage, decent pay, and if you survived twenty years of service, a pension at half pay. We completed our police purchases near the end of the day and went our separate ways, reminding each other to wear our new recruit training uniforms to class the next morning!

I still had to run over to the Chief Magistrate's office to resign my court officer position. I wanted to be sure I was accepted for the Transit Police Department before resigning my court officer position. I turned my court officer's shield into the chief court clerk (who later became the Chief Magistrate) and told him I was resigning to accept a higher paying position in the Transit Police Department. He said he was sorry to lose me as I had been a good court officer, and was well-regarded by my bosses and my fellow officers. He wished me luck in my new job and added that I could come back to the courts if I didn't like the new job. I thanked him very much and wished him well. He was a really nice guy, particularly for a boss!

I had one more stop to make on the way home – to the court at 161st Street in the Bronx to say goodbye to my co-workers. It was a tough thing to do. My nine months of service as a court officer in the Bronx Court had been interesting and happy ones. I had learned a lot about the criminal justice system, and a lot about people. I left that job grateful for the opportunity to have been a court officer, and sad because I no longer would be working with such fine people. Everyone wished me luck, fond farewells were made, and I hopped the crosstown bus for the ride home. Tomorrow was the dawn of a new day, and a new career!

Chapter 3

A letter arrived that day informing us that we had been accepted as tenants by the Eastchester Housing Project. Eileen and I were thrilled at the news since we had been living with relatives since moving out of our place in Washington Heights, shuttling back and forth between my mother's house in the Bronx and Eileen's cousin's house in Astoria. Both houses were really overcrowded and didn't really have the room to accommodate us. Still, they let us stay until we could get a place of our own. We moved into a brand new apartment on Yates Avenue in the Bronx in January 1950. It was a neat little apartment with two and a half rooms, located on the ground floor. The rent, including gas and electric, was $54 per month – very reasonable at the time. Just about all of the tenants in the building were about our ages, with one or two kids. And most of the men were veterans, so we had a lot in common. Everyone got along well. We had many good times together and formed a few long-term friendships as well.

The family that lived across the hall from us had the

first TV set in the building. The husband, Frank, was in the undertaker business and had to remain on call at home to receive his job assignments. Owning a TV set was a great way for Frank to manage his time between calls. But Frank, his wife Molly, and their three children were kind enough to share their TV with many of us in the building. I'm afraid we all took advantage of their generosity, cramming in to the apartment while watching "Uncle Milty," "Lights Out," and all the fights! They even served us coffee and cake. Thank God, before long, most of us bought our own sets. What a relief for Frank's family!

During my time watching TV at Frank's, I was going through the New York City Police Academy as a transit police recruit. I had all day hours with most Saturdays and Sundays off. That's how I managed to get in all that TV time! The Academy days flew by much too quickly, filled with excitement and hard work. From the very first day we reported to the old Police Academy Building at #7 Hubert Street in downtown Manhattan, we knew that our lives would never be the same again. To begin with, the Police Academy didn't really look like a police academy, at least not one befitting a big department like the NYPD. This was the world's largest police department, I might add. The building was located in a very old -- and probably condemned -- public school. The building was about six stories high, with our class located on the top floor. Since all recruits were required to walk up the stairs when going to classes, we were kept in pretty good shape -- more than could be said for that building! Paint was peeling off the ceilings and walls, the sad green shades were either torn or had holes in them. The old iron radiators rattled with steam hissing out, and the lights were very dim. Despite such Spartan surroundings, the course material and the caliber of the instructors were excellent and they prepared us well for our future careers in law enforcement. The class instructors were all lieutenants and most of them had a good sense of humor, which greatly helped them get their lessons across. They almost always laced their lessons with cop stories drawn from their police experiences. No matter what the subject was -- penal law, criminal procedure law, administrative code, or the manual of procedure -- cop stories would be told to help solidify the lesson's main points. It was a very effective way to teach, and since as recruits we really had no idea what it was like to be a police officer, they always had our attention.

The instructors meant so much to us, and it was important that we relate to them in ways that other students did not have to relate to their teachers. For they were not just preparing us for the business world; they were preparing us for a real-life battle against crime. Lieutenant "G" was one instructor who stood out. He was a master at telling cop stories and was a terrific teacher. I can vividly recall one such lesson. The subject was public morals, which in 1950 had a definite Victorian flair compared with present day standards. "When I was a desk officer in the 13th Precinct on East 35th Street," said the lieutenant, "I had to interview many male complainants who had just rushed up the station house stairs from waiting taxis. These guys would sort of crouch down in front of the massive desk while relating the details of their complaint. The reason these men were crouching is because they had no pants on! They were mostly out of town business men looking for a little female companionship. They had been approached by a prostitute on the street and hustled into some hallway where a male accomplice, usually their pimp, was waiting for the 'John' to appear. Once the John and the gal were in the hallway beginning to get intimate, the pimp would pull out a weapon and announce a stick-up. He would then take the John's wallet and other valuables, and then force the John to remove his pants. The pimp and the prostitute would then take off, leaving the John in the hallway, at half mast so to speak. It usually took several minutes for the shock to wear off and for them to face up to going out on the streets, in a city they were just visiting, without pants on and hoping they could wave down a cab driver who would believe their story and drive them to the nearest police station. By this time, the pimp and the prostitute were long gone and another 'Murphy Game' had been successfully concluded! Usually, when the John got to the police station, he had conjured up a story of his own on how he had been mugged by a bunch of guys armed with guns and knives. He would completely leave out the details about the pimp and the prostitute for these Johns usually had wives who wouldn't appreciate the details of the true story. Unfortunately, the version given by these Johns didn't help police efforts to apprehend the culprits."

"Of course, the cops suspected what had really happened," continued the lieutenant, "and after a few minutes of interrogation by the precinct detectives, the real facts emerged, but only after the John had received assurance that everything would be kept confidential, with no calls being made to his wife or company officials. The detectives would then go to work obtaining a description, and the modus operandi, of the suspects. Usually, a decoy cop would then pose as an out-of-towner looking for some action. The decoy cop would be backed up by his partner as a loose tail. It didn't take long for the bait to be taken, with the decoy cop being led into a certain hallway to be held up by the lurking accomplice. It was standard procedure to give up the money, which was marked for evidence, and let the pair escape – momentarily. The decoy cop's partner was waiting outside, having selected a spot that afforded him coverage and that presented no danger to any passersby in the event of gunplay. There usually wasn't any shooting because the pimp didn't know that the John was a decoy cop, and for obvious reasons, he figured the John wouldn't appear in court and the case would be thrown out. Imagine his surprise when he learned just who his gal's customer really was!"

When the lieutenant completed his story, we recruits had a good mental picture of the characters, their roles, police methods used to solve these crimes, how to deal with complaining citizens, and what sections of the penal law were violated. And that's the way it went at the Academy, regardless of the crime being discussed. Stories such as these proved to be great teaching tools.

In addition to these classes conducted at #7 Hubert Street, we also had to attend several sessions of firearms training. Since the Police Department ranges were located at either a National Guard Armory or Army Reserve location, or in one case, a city high school, it was necessary to travel from the Academy to different areas of the city. It generally followed that if you had firearms training in the morning, you had classes at Hubert Street in the afternoon. Or you were scheduled for physical training at yet another armory in the Bronx. Physical training took place about five times a week. It seemed like we were constantly scurrying back and forth on subways in our green recruit uniforms, carrying our little bags with our books, sneakers, flashlights, nightsticks, guns, etc. Trying to be on time for our various classes, while squeezing in a bite to eat and avoiding making any minor arrests, was a challenge. Most of the citizens had no idea who we were. They probably thought we were a bunch of Marine recruits who lost their way in the subways of the "Big City."

Firearms training started on our very first day at the Academy, and although most of us were service veterans, very few of us knew anything about police revolvers. Our initial instructions consisted of presenting our unloaded revolvers to the Range Sergeant for inspection, barrels pointed downward, cylinders opened. After each officer's weapon was inspected and tested by weights for proper trigger pull, we were given thirty rounds of ammunition. We were then assigned to firing points on the firing line, the old Army "L" type targets were swung into place, and each officer was instructed to load five rounds into the chamber and standby for slow fire. At the command "Ready on the right; ready on the left; all ready on the firing line," we hopefully had our weapons aimed in the general direction of the targets. Then a whistle blew and we commenced firing – some bullets hit the ceiling, some hit the target pulley lines, some hit the walls, and in a few rare instances, some hit the intended target! My first shot went clear through the opening of the steel arm that held up the target, leaving it hanging "naked" for all to see. The shot was about one foot higher than and one foot to the right of where it was supposed to go. Undaunted, I proceeded to put the next four rounds in various and sundry locations – just about everywhere but the target. After persistent yelling by the range officers to "watch your sights; squeeze the trigger," we started to hit some targets as we went through our other firing paces: ten rounds of slow fire, ten rounds of timed fire, and ten rounds of rapid fire. At that point, we reloaded for street wear with six rounds, holstered our weapons, and reported for more verbal instructions on the care and safety of handling revolvers.

We left the range fully aware of the revolver's awesome ability to kill, and I left there with the fervent hope that I would never have to use it for that purpose. We were all aware of the trust and responsibility placed in each of us. What a burden – particularly when you realize that a police officer in a dark alley, or in a dark subway passageway, in a confrontation with a felon who allegedly just committed a violent crime, has to make a split-second decision about whether or not to use deadly force. If deadly force is used, the police officer's actions may then be reviewed by the court, where a learned judge or judges, with all the law books conveniently at hand, and in the cold light of a Monday morning, determines if the officer's actions were justified. There is no mistaking a police officer's responsibility.

The physical training classes were something else and the physical training staff was commanded by a Lieutenant "B," a real martinet. He wore a regulation Army shirt with police blue pants. He was assisted by three sergeants – one had been a contender for the Mr. America title, one was an ex-Golden Glover, and one was an ex-Marine drill instructor! These physical classes were tough with all the push-ups, sit-ups, running board jumps, and tumblesaults. We were also given boxing lessons, training in the proper use of the nightstick, Judo lessons, and plenty of marching. In short, we did just about everything but walk around the gym floor, on our knees, on broken glass!

The facilities at the gym, located in the armory, were not the best. There were no lockers or showers for us recruits. We simply changed from our street clothes into our gym outfits up in the balcony, and left our gear on the empty seats. We then went down on the gym floor and went through our paces, which always resulted in plenty of sweat.

Following that, we changed back into our recruit uniforms, washed our hands and faces, combed our hair, and reported for inspection before being dismissed. I felt sorry for the inspecting officer having to do the inspections at close quarters – all before spray deodorants were even manufactured! One thing that did help though, were the many broken windows in the place. The cold winter breezes certainly helped clear the air. We didn't have any problem getting seats on the subway either – everybody gave us a wide berth.

A strange incident happened one time at the gym, probably due to the fact that we had no lockers and had to leave our stuff on empty seats. The way I remember it, one of the guys in the class had to go back upstairs to get something. He noticed his wallet was missing and reported the loss to the lieutenant in charge. The lieutenant immediately called us all to formation and announced that someone had taken someone else's wallet. He demanded that the culprit step forward and take his medicine, which of course, was immediate dismissal from the force and, quite possibly, jail time. Naturally, no one stepped forward. The lieutenant went on about detectives being called in and everybody being searched and so forth. Still, no one moved. The lieutenant then had another idea. "I'm going to declare a short break and ask everyone to conduct a search for the missing property. Maybe someone will find it on the floor or some other place that has been overlooked." And wouldn't you know someone found the wallet on the floor, just under a radiator. The incident was resolved without any further action. For a long time afterward, I pondered whether someone had taken the wallet, or if it had just fallen on the floor. I don't know if justice was really served, but at least the guy got his wallet back intact!

Overall, the physical training was good and it got us into shape. The sergeants were really fantastic guys and they worked hard with the troops. In police work, and any other line of work for that matter, the first line supervisors and the "troops" really get the job done. Once you advance above that rank, it's very difficult to maintain the kind of close contact that gets the best results. Lieutenant B was merely an authority figure to us, who usually chewed us out at roll calls or who "zapped" us for forgetting our memo books or flashlights. I now understand that he had other important administrative functions to perform that we recruits were just not aware of at the time.

One of the minor irritants we transit cops had to put up with while attending the New York City Police Academy were the taunts and innuendos. "Can you guys carry a gun?" "Can you make an arrest outside the subway?" "Why don't you become a real cop?" The informal replies to these questions were usually hostile, and barracks-like. But as to the correct answers to those same questions: "Yes we can carry a gun, both on- and off- duty." And, "As members of a duly constituted police department, we have full police powers and must make an arrest for any crime committed in our presence, anywhere in the State of New York." And finally, "Yes, transit cops are real cops!" Such comments from some

NYPD cops and civilians just had to be accepted as part of the job, caused by the fact that the City of New York insists on maintaining three separate police forces – the city police, the housing police, and the transit police. Despite the recommendations of several fact- finding committees to merge these three departments in order to remove the duplication, unify command, and fix responsibility – all in the public interest – it has not happened. [1] Of course, today, there is far less friction, vastly improved cooperation, more mutual respect, and better understanding of each department's role. Such understanding simply didn't exist when I was a recruit!

---

[1] Editor's Note: In 1995, the three forces were fully integrated into one and now all members proudly display the emblem of the NYPD. I am confident that Dad's many efforts to effect this change played a part in making it actually happen. And I am very happy that he lived to see it. He wore his "NYPD" cap proudly, while never forgetting his roots as a transit cop.

Chapter 4

At the end of our eight-week training stint at the Police Academy, we graduated and were assigned to full police duty at one of the eight police districts. Since I lived in the Bronx at the time, I was assigned to District #4 located at 180th Street, near the Bronx Zoo. I reported there for my first midnight-to-eight tour on a bitter cold night in February, carrying with me my brand new uniforms. I was immediately disappointed when I saw the police headquarters. It was located in a very small room on the 2nd floor, near the Signal Tower. The outgoing platoon consisted of four cops, including me. The other guys were old timers from the "Old Sod" and they were not overly friendly or helpful to this recruit that first tour. I dressed in silence, listening to such comments as, "Are you going to the hurling game at Coke Park this Sunday, Dan?" or, "Jim, are you going to visit the old country again this summer?" Jim had the Home Post, which included the old Dyre Avenue shuttle -- a deserted, rural "Tuneyville Choo Choo" in those days. A look at the roll call told me that my post was the entire White Plains Road line, from Jackson Avenue North to 241st Street. There was no sergeant assigned to turn out the platoon, so at midnight, Jim, the Home Post officer, simply said, "Out you go, lads." "By the way, Martin," Jim said, "make sure you get rid of the bums at the end of the line. Put them down on the street and watch out that the city cops don't put them back on the subway. Tell those city cops, 'This ain't no hotel, it's a railroad!'"

We went our separate ways and started our patrols. I took the first northbound train, and after the doors closed, started walking through the train feeling very self-conscious in my brand-new uniform. I tried to appear nonchalant as I twirled my nightstick while whistling the tune "Peg of my Heart." I escaped from the first train without incident, de-training at the next station and proceeding to inspect the platforms, thinking to myself, "What other stupid ass would be out on a bitter cold morning if he wasn't paid for it?" I soon learned that plenty of people were always out at night on the subway system, regardless of the weather. Almost all of them were there for legitimate reasons – going to/from work, returning from a party, visiting a friend, and so forth. Only a small percentage of people used the subway system to commit crimes. Of course, there were the homeless, drift-ers, and other lost souls who virtually lived in the subways. It was part of the patrol officer's duties to "take necessary and appropriate police action," whatever the hell that means, in connection with these derelicts. Most times it meant mov-ing them off the post, but sometimes, you just couldn't get them moved because they preferred to be locked up! If arrested, they would at least get cleaned up, fed, and be given a place to sleep, at least for the night. These types of arrests never made a hit with the desk officers, the courts, or the Department of Corrections, who were responsible for housing them after sentence was imposed. Almost all of these people were in a pretty bad state -- filthy dirty, a bit smelly, and some were infested with lice. So processing them was a rather unpleasant task. No one greeted the arresting officer warmly! After a short time "in the can," these poor souls would return to the subways, and the vicious cycle would begin again.

Apropos of this problem with the homeless, some twenty-nine years after that first midnight patrol in the Bronx, while serving as commanding officer of the 3rd Transit Police District, I was still trying to cope with the issue. One day, I received a buck slip from the chief which was attached to a copy of a letter he had received. The letter complained about the deplorable, unsightly, and unsanitary conditions caused by derelicts urinating, defecating, and sleeping on the trains and station benches – particularly at terminal stations such as 207th Street on the "A" line. The writer demanded action and the chief directed that I "take necessary and appropriate action." So here is how I handled it. I assigned one of my "heavy hitters" to the task: a cop nicknamed "Dirty Harry" by his cohorts. I instructed him to address the issue with the derelicts at the 207th Street station. But I neglected to mention a specific number. So, Dirty Harry did his own math and came up with about twenty "bumming arrests." Well, you can imagine the consternation it created throughout the local criminal justice system! Just picture the scene. Here comes Officer Dirty Harry, with his twenty scratching derelicts in tow, into the serene surroundings of the 34th Precinct Police Station. He stands before the desk officer with this ripe group, who by then was staring in disbelief, after spilling his coffee all over the blotter! "What the hell is this, officer?" asks the desk officer, "are you for real? What idiot ordered these arrests? We don't even have cells in this precinct! Where the hell am I going to put them? What's your captain's name and phone number?" The poor lieutenant rattled on and on. Dirty Harry, who happened to be a very bright and highly qualified officer and fluent in about four languages, informed the lieutenant that such arrests were ordered by his captain in response to a public demand, directed further by orders from his chief to take "necessary and appropriate police action." The lieutenant's answer to that was a direct order to Dirty Harry to get the people somewhere else in the building, anywhere but there – away from the desk area – and get started on the necessary paperwork.

I received a prompt phone call from Captain "G," the precinct commander, asking in essence, "Why did you do this to my command?" He let me know that two gallons of ammonia and one gallon of Clorox bleach had already been dispensed with no appreciable results. He also wanted to know if I could send additional manpower to assist in processing the prisoners. I assured him that these arrests were not likely to become a common occurrence because we hoped for positive results by discouraging these derelicts through the arrest process. I agreed to send three officers to assist Dirty Harry with the paperwork, and to get the derelicts out of the precinct forthwith! I then spent a good part of that day on the phone trying to arrange transport to court. When I informed the wagon master of the type of clientele to be transported, I received all kinds of excuses as to why no vehicles were available. "Gee Cap, we have heavy runs to several precincts and won't have a wagon available for several hours," said the wagon master. "Can't you use your own radio cars, or maybe get hold of a Transit Authority bus?" It took a call to the borough chief to finally come up with a wagon.

Since by now it was already late afternoon, everyone had to be held for night court. When they finally arrived at night court, the courts and the Department of Corrections refused to accept them until they had been deloused and bathed. More calls were made – to Bellevue Hospital, who refused to delouse, and to the Men's Shelter, who also refused to delouse. We reached the top person in charge at the Men's Shelter and he ordered that the derelicts be accepted. By this time, about sixteen hours had elapsed and the news media was beginning to give the matter a lot of play. Another fourteen hours go by and Dirty Harry finally gets his prisoners arraigned. The derelicts have all been deloused, received baths, been issued clean clothes, and have gotten a decent night's sleep in a bed. The court issues them a stern warning regarding the ills of using the subway as a hotel and they are released. What else could the judge do?

So, in review, let's take a look at the plusses:

1. I took "necessary and appropriate action."
2. We got the 34th Precinct a huge steel cell made out of old subway railings, making the precinct captain and his officers very happy.
3. Officer Dirty Harry got some thirty hours of overtime. Incidentally, Dirty Harry had a business on the side, so the overtime pay was much appreciated. His side business – exterminating!
4. The derelicts all got a night's sleep in a clean bed plus clean clothes, a hot meal, and as a bonus, the cops threw in packs of cigarettes!

A big headline appeared in the *Daily News* proclaiming, "THIS TRIP WAS A BUMMER" and the accompanying story contained a detailed account of the entire incident. After that caper, I never got any more of those buck slips from the chief directing me to take "necessary and appropriate police action"!

Chapter 5

I would like to go back to that first night on patrol in the Bronx so many years ago when I was still a rookie cop. After inspecting the station platforms, I next checked the mezzanine and the toilets. The toilets had to be inspected at every station frequently as they were often crime hazard locations. After making sure that no one was loitering in the toilets, I approached the token booth to chat with the clerk on duty. Since the trains ran every twenty minutes in those days during the late hours, I could safely spare a few minutes talking with the clerk. The clerks were happy to see a cop because it lessened their fears of a holdup. It also reduced the likelihood of their being verbally assaulted by a nasty drunk. And it helped pass the time for them. I heard the next train approaching, so I bid the clerk goodbye, calling over my shoulder as I ran upstairs to the train, "Maybe I'll see you later on." I let him know that I was heading for the Gun Hill Road station. I boarded the train and started my patrol, going into my whistle and night stick twirling routine. Feeling a little like Phil Reagan, the former singing cop, I entered the second car in the train. It was quite crowded, but I noticed that several persons were standing even though there were some empty seats still available. Then I saw why! Seated in the middle of six empty seats was a poor old homeless woman. Her clothes were ragged and dirty. She had several sores on both legs and the odor that surrounded her was definitely not Chanel #5. The situation called for action on my part as the other passengers looked at me with pleading eyes.

I put my best foot forward and cheerily greeted the homeless woman, "Good Morning, ma'am," – a throwback to my training with Aunt May. "Do you live in the area?" I asked.

"None of your f------- business," she replied.

I countered with, "Ma'am, that's not a nice way for a refined person such as yourself to talk. Where do you live?" She then let out a flood of profanity that made even the sailor in me blush.

Everyone in the train car appeared to be enjoying the show between the old gal and the rookie cop. I was mentally groping for a gracious way out of the dilemma so that I could retreat with dignity. But the lady just wouldn't give up. The train continued on its way making stops at every station, and at every station stop, I prayed she would get off. No such luck. She was going to ride to the end of the line and continue to blast this rookie all the way. My repeated requests for identification fell on deaf ears, and so did my gentle reminder that she was violating the law by her disorderly actions. She even blew off my strong order to desist these disorderly actions or I would have to place her under arrest. Luckily for me, the train finally reached the last stop and the remaining passengers hurriedly left the train, leaving just the two of us to work things out. Now, I dropped the "ma'am" stuff and spoke to her in language more her style. She seemed to respect this change in my demeanor and after a few more salty exchanges, she retreated to the street below – probably to have coffee and to break the chops of some unfortunate counterperson. I never saw her again, but she certainly gave me a quick on-the-job training lesson in public relations!

The rest of that first midnight patrol tour passed rather quickly since I had so many stations to patrol. By 3:30 a.m., hardly anyone was riding the subway except for a few late drinkers just turned out of the bars. I gave them special attention since most of them were likely to fall asleep and then they would become easy prey for the pickpockets. By waking them, or just by staying in the train car with them, I was keeping down crime on my post.

For those of you who do not know it, the subways are a favorite hunting ground for "lush workers," a type of thief without much class. Lush workers roll drunks, sometimes using a razor blade to slit the pockets of sleeping victims. The real pickpockets are known as "cannons." These thieves have savoir faire and can pick a person's pocket in a crowd without the victim realizing it. Another type of larceny thief is called a "bag opener." These characters are adept at opening the clasp on a pocketbook and removing the wallet or change purse without the victim knowing it. Then you have the "bag snatch," "necklace snatch," "hat snatch," or "watch snatch" – creeps who simply snatch the items from victims and flee. Most of these are youths, wear sneakers, and are very fast, agile, and don't give a damn if they injure their victims. And given their style of attack, they often do cause injuries. Many times, these thieves ride between the train cars and simply reach out and grab a bag right off the person's arm as the train enters or leaves the station. Sometimes, the victim clings to the bag and is dragged down the platform and knocked against one of the steel support columns, resulting in serious or fatal injuries. This is certainly not child's play. And yet, some of these kids actually start playing such deadly games when they are only eight years old! Sometimes, these kids lean too far in reaching for a bag and fall from the moving train, resulting in either death or the certain loss of limbs. Cops never get used to such gory and tragic sights, and yet they see a lot of them. This is why I was giving the sleeping drunks special attention that first night on patrol.

I took my meal around 4:30 a.m. that first shift at the West Farms Road station since there were a few all-night restaurants located there. I decided on Bickford's mainly because it was the cheapest. I went in there feeling a little self-conscious in my brand-new uniform, heading for an empty table in the rear. There were coat hooks on the wall and I promptly hung both my uniform coat and cap on them, only to reveal my green-and-white reindeer-embroidered wool sweater. I figured this to be the in thing for cops to wear under their uniform coats, and it served as my visual signal to everyone in the restaurant that I was temporarily off-duty. But it didn't have quite the desired effect since I still had on uniform pants and my gun belt and revolver. I sauntered up to the food counter and ordered scrambled eggs, home fries, and coffee. When I offered to pay, the guy behind the cash register asked, "Are you from the 48th precinct?"

"No," I said, "I'm a transit cop."

"Transit -- oh, I see," he replied, and rang up $.60. I paid and as I returned to my seat and started to eat my meal, I kept thinking about our exchange. Little did I realize it at the time, but his response was typical of what I would hear over the next thirty years. You could be off-duty and out socially with friends.

"What type of work do you do, John?" someone would ask.

"I'm a police officer."

"Great, what precinct are you in?"

"I'm a transit cop."

"Transit -- oh, I see. I thought you were a real cop."

"What's a real cop?" I would ask.

"A city cop," he would reply. I would then launch into a lengthy explanation concerning the police powers and duties of a transit police officer. This explanation included the shocker that transit cops could make arrests and take police action not only in the subways, but anywhere in the State of New York in the lawful performance of their duties. I would often go on to make the following analogies, "Ted Williams surely is a major league ball player, even though he doesn't play for the New York Yankees." And, "Just because a milkman works for Borden's doesn't mean he's a real milkman and the guy that works for Queens Dairy isn't." Maybe these weren't the best examples to give, but it was the way I put it. After a while, I stopped trying to explain and just tried to live with it as sort of a job condition. Look, the Marines are for real, but so are the Army, the Navy, the Coast Guard, and the Air Force. Likewise, City, Transit, Housing, County, State, Federal, Parkways, Towns, Villages, and Parks – they are all real cops.

So, back to my breakfast at Bickford's that first night of my patrol. I was sipping my second cup of coffee and carefully avoiding the stares of some of the customers when I noticed two city cops enter the restaurant. They went to the counter, got their food, and sat down at a table opposite me. "How's it going?" they asked.

"OK," I said.

"Are you from the precinct?"

"No, I'm from transit."

"Transit -- oh."

But one of the cops then said, "That's a good job. How do you like it?"

"I like it so far. This is actually my first night on the job."

"Don't sweat it, kid -- in a week's time, you'll be a pro and within a year, you'll have seen everything. After that, it's a repeat. It's a ringside seat at the greatest show on earth!" The three of us chatted on for the next ten minutes like old war buddies. No class distinction, just three cops taking a break. As I was leaving, they said, "Good luck. See you around and don't forget, we are on the air if you need help." I felt good resuming patrol. I liked the easy way I was accepted by the city cops – it eased my mind, and that chip on my shoulder.

It was now 5:00 a.m. as I was climbing the stairs up to the mezzanine where the token booth was located. I made my "ring" – "Patrolman Martin, back on post from meal." The desk sergeant advised me to keep warm and keep patrolling. I pondered how I could do both since it was about 2 °F above zero and those open, elevated platforms were cold as "Kelsey's balls." I thought back to my days aboard a destroyer in the Bering Sea off the Aleutian Islands, and immediately felt much warmer. The early work crowd was starting to enter the transit system en route to their jobs downtown, so I had plenty of company for the rest of my tour. Suddenly, a call came across the radio – "man under a train!"

The incident occurred at the 210th Street station of the old 3rd Avenue "El" which, incidentally, was not part of my post. Regardless, I got the assignment. Some poor soul decided to pack it in by diving in front of a northbound train. I was the first officer on the scene and I think I automatically did everything they taught us at the Police Academy. I jumped down on the tracks and walked to where the lower half of the body was resting. I assisted the transit workers in removing the remains to the station platform, after which I busied myself getting the card numbers of the train; the car numbers of the train cars that passed over the victim; the names, pass numbers, and run numbers of the motorman and conductor, plus their statements; the names, addresses, telephone numbers, and statements of several witnesses; the name, shield numbers, and commands of the city police on the scene; the name of the hospital, telephone number, and the name of the doctor in attendance (in those days); the trainmaster's name , number, time the power was turned off and on and by whom. By the time the other half of the body was recovered from the street area below, searched, and possible identification established, it was well past 9:00 a.m.

I still had to get back to my command and submit my report. It took me until after 11:00 a.m. to do the report, go off duty, and head for home. My wife, Eileen, was already a nervous wreck figuring something horrible had happened to me on my very first night of patrol. When she opened the door in response to my knock and saw me, she gave me a big hug and kiss, and then put the coffee and toast on. We discussed the very first tour, laughing at the funny parts and becoming somber over my "man under" story. It's a funny thing, but after telling my wife about that first tour, we rarely discussed what happened on the job in such detail again. Perhaps we just became veterans that very first night and never felt the need to discuss things in detail again.

I jumped right into bed after breakfast and in a short time, fell fast asleep -- not without wondering, however, why I got sent on the "man under" assignment when it did not occur on my post. I concluded that it was because the old Irish cop who had the post was fearful of submitting written reports. And I found out later on that my theory was correct. The guy hated to write, even a simple "aided card." I didn't like working with that guy since the sergeant would farm his work out to me. Since I was just a rookie I couldn't squawk too much to the sergeant, but I let the cop know how I felt. After a while, I learned how to manage to be on some other police condition when something happened on his post.

Thank God my stay in District #4 was short-lived – it lasted only four months. I put in for a transfer to District #1, the most active district we had. Although it meant forty-five minutes more travel a day, I was happy when the transfer came through. District #1 was located at the 57th Street station on the Westside of mid-Manhattan, one of the busiest parts of New York City. Several of the guys from my class at the Police Academy were already assigned there, and the "older" officers were really not that much older than us rookies. Most of the "older" guys had also served in the armed forces, so we all related and functioned well together. There was always lots of laughter and horsing around in the locker room before going on or off duty. Cop stories abounded freely, which added to the learning process.

Many a night after a 4:00 p.m.-to-midnight tour, several of us would stop off for a few brews at our favorite watering hole, to swap cop stories and unwind a bit. I guess we were an early version of "The Choirboys" of the LAPD. Somewhat tamer maybe, but with similar symptoms! We just weren't lucky enough to get a particular lieutenant in a compromising situation like The Choirboys did! We didn't have a "Sperm Whale Whalen" in the group either, but we did have Officer Irwin K, and he was quite a character. He was a bachelor who had actually worked in the circus at one time. Irwin could also play the piano quite well and many a time he provided the musical accompaniment to our vocal efforts at the watering hole. His personal hygiene left a lot to be desired, so we gave him plenty of space in the locker room. He never seemed to have his own cigarettes, so we posted the following sign in the head. "PLEASE DO NOT DISCARD CIGARETTE BUTTS IN THE URINALS AS THEY GET WET AND MAKE IT DIFFICULT FOR IRWIN TO IGNITE." Despite his personal habits, we all liked Irwin and he liked us.

However, Irwin was somewhat inflexible in enforcing minor law violations. I was in night court one hot summer evening waiting to arraign my prisoner when the door leading to the detention area sprung open. Officer K popped out carrying in his arms a legless guy who was still sitting on his little cart, complete with his box of pencils. Irwin had his uniform cap off revealing his completely shaved head, which seemed to make the large wart on his nose stand out even further. Remember, this was before Yul Brynner and Telly Savalas made shaved heads popular! The crowd in the courtroom broke up at the sight of Irwin and his desperate prisoner. It took the Judge about ten minutes of constant gravel pounding to restore order. Whereupon Officer K placed his prisoner and the cart on the floor before the arraigning magistrate while the court officer read the charge. It stated, in substance, "You are charged with unlawfully peddling pencils in the Times Square IRT subway station." The judge asked Irwin why he hadn't just issued a summons instead of arresting the man. Irwin informed the judge that the man refused to give the proper identification, became loud and boisterous, and further, several passengers complained about the peddler's abusive conduct.

"Couldn't you have shown some compassion and just ejected him from the subway? After all, he is a cripple," said the judge.

"Your Honor," replied Irwin, "I deal in violations, not personalities." Whereupon the judge found the peddler guilty, gave him a suspended sentence, and directed Irwin to return him to the nearest subway. The crowd in the courtroom loudly applauded the judge's decision and booed poor Irwin as he carried his charge out of the court. But Officer K left smiling. After all, he did what he had to do. As it turned out, the cripple was a real buster and most cops, including me, would have taken the easy way out and more or less ignored the situation. But not Irwin!

A few months after this incident, we were all shocked to

read the following headline in the *Daily News:* "OFFICER SHOT AND KILLED BY GIRLFRIEND." The details of the story indicated that Officer Irwin K of the Transit Police Department was shot five times by a lady friend who shared an apartment with him. It seemed she became jealous of Irwin's attentions toward another female. She did not have movie queen looks, but neither was Irwin exactly a Cary Grant.

Things really quieted down after that with the 4-to-12 watering hole group and not only because of Irwin's sudden demise. Most of the 300 of us rookies appointed to the transit police at the time were on other civil service lists, such as the city police list and the fire department list. Every month, guys were leaving for the "PD" or "FD." Within about a year, some 150 guys had left, mainly because the benefits were much better in those two jobs. The pay difference between the jobs was only about $150 a year, but the difference in the other benefits was significant. The PD and FD offered a twenty-year retirement plan, unlimited sick leave, better vacations, and certainly, more prestige. The Transit Police Department lost 150 good members, many of whom went on to become high- ranking officers in those departments. The 150 of us who remained with the transit police vowed we would seek job benefits equivalent to those of the city police. It was only right.

Chapter 6

It was about that time that I decided to run for office in our Patrolman's Benevolent Association *(PBA)* in order to help attain our goals. I was appointed second vice president of the PBA, vacant at the time, and I immediately jumped into action. Our bosses consisted of one captain and seven acting captains, all on loan from the City Police Department, and assigned to command the Transit Police Department. These bosses decided that our uniforms were too identical to the city police and determined that we should wear a distinguishing shoulder patch. Someone designed the weirdest-looking patch and the guys on the job did not like it at all. The patch was a large "T" made from light blue, cheap cloth material with bright red *(closer to pink)* lettering that said "New York City Transit Police." The patch had to be sewn on the left shoulder of our uniforms and when the guys saw the order, they went berserk. It became a catalyst for them. "Hey, John, what is the PBA doing about this damn patch?" "Let's fight this crazy order." "Let's get rid of these PD jerks and get our own bosses." And so it went.

I contacted the PBA president, who informed me that he had fought the patch issue already and had obtained a partial victory. The bosses had originally wanted us to wear two patches, one on each shoulder. He added that he could do no more at the present time. I didn't agree with our president and told him that I would continue the fight my own way to have the patch removed. I wasn't against wearing a patch, but I wanted one that would enhance the image of the department, for example, a patch circular in design and worn in a standard location – on the center of the left arm – similar to those worn by traffic cops or Port Authority cops. The patch issue was important to the patrolmen and I vowed to get the "T" replaced. It took a year, but I finally succeeded. Here's how I managed it.

First, I made an appointment to see our commanding officer, the captain from the city police. I knew he would not agree with a change in patches, but I wanted to go through channels before going over his head. I showed up for the appointment in the uniform of the day, with the "T" on my left shoulder as required. However, instead of being sewn on, I had Scotch tape affixed to the back of the patch and the tape held the patch in place! You see, after I stood formation for roll calls, off would come the patch and I'd stick it in the back of my memo book until I went off duty. It was my way of not complying with the order. It was risky, and somewhat insubordinate, but that's what I did as my form of protest to what I considered an unlawful order.

As I concluded my meeting with the captain, at which he stoutly refused to rescind the order concerning the patch despite my pitch about morale, he patted my left shoulder in a parting gesture. To his surprise, the Scotch taped "T" came off my shirt and landed in his hand. The captain had high blood pressure to begin with and I thought he was going to have a stroke. I mean, he really flipped. "You're out of uniform! I ought to give you a complaint. You're defying a lawful order. Why wasn't that patch sewn on?" The captain finally ordered me out of his office and as a parting shot, vowed that the patch was here to stay. It was difficult for me to keep from laughing, but I managed. As I was about to walk through the door – the door the captain had opened after the patch came off in his hand – I turned around to face the boss. I then said, "Sir, I hereby put you on official notice that I shall pursue this matter with the chief executive officer of the Transit Authority." The captain then bid me good day, adding a grim reminder that I make sure I patrol my post in a most diligent manner. I knew I definitely had not made a hit with the captain!

On my next set of day tours, I was fortunate enough to be assigned to a post at the 34th Street and Broadway station of the BMT subway. It was a very busy station and was therefore a fixed post. The two big department stores, Macy's and Gimble's, in addition to dozens of small shops, were located at that station. The famous Empire State Building was also located in close vicinity of that station, which was where the newly appointed chief executive officer of the Transit Authority had an office. He was a retired Army general who was also vice president of a huge liquor company, a position he held in addition to his job as chief executive officer of the Transit Authority. I decided to visit him and seek his approval in removing the patch which, by the way, was still Scotch taped to my uniform. I walked the one block from the subway to the general's office, answering about twenty questions from people en route. "Pardon me, Officer. Where is Macy's?" "Which way is the Empire State Building?" "How do I get to Penn Station?" I finally made it to the inside of the Empire State Building, went to the directory, and located the floor number of the general's office. I took the elevator to the 40th floor, got off, sauntered into his office, and approached the receptionist.

"Good morning, ma'am," (my Aunt May training again.) "My name is Patrolman Martin of the transit police. I do not have an appointment, but I would like to see General Casey if he is available." The young lady invited me to have a seat and then she entered another office. After only a few moments, the receptionist returned, accompanied by a distinguished-looking gentleman. A Hollywood casting director must have cast him for his many real life roles – Army general, vice president of a big corporation, chief executive officer of the Transit Authority. The general had white hair and a neatly trimmed mustache to top off his trim military posture. He extended his hand, introduced himself, and invited me into his office.

"Please sit down, Officer. How about a cup of coffee?"

Two cups were immediately sent in. I took my first gulp and pondered how to begin to explain my mission, which seemed, in such surroundings, to have paled a bit. Hell, I thought, it's important or I wouldn't be here in the first place with my butt on the line! Why else would I be sticking my tail out by intruding on a general, and going off post to boot?

"General," I began, "I'm sorry to intrude on your valuable time, and forgive me for not calling for an appointment beforehand. The reason I'm here concerns a very serious morale and esprit de corps problem regarding the men I represent." I figured these terms would get the general's attention. "I don't believe it is too difficult to resolve if reasonable men put their minds to it." I then related the entire "patch story," including my meeting with the captain. I proposed that a new, circular patch be designed. The patch should be blue and gold in color with the wording "New York City Transit Police" around the edge of the circle and with the New York City Transit Authority insignia in the center. Such a patch would clearly distinguish our members from those of other agencies, and would be acceptable to the men. The general heard me out and promised to look into the matter and get back to me in a couple of weeks. He indicated that he would discuss the matter with my captain and other executive members of the Transit Authority. When leaving the general's office, I mentioned that the guys in my command district were giving a Christmas party for a group of underprivileged children at Roosevelt Hospital the next week. I invited the general, and to my surprise, he agreed to come to the party.

I floated on air through the crowds while returning to my post, and was greatly relieved to learn that nothing unusual happened during my absence. The cop covering the IND station had covered my post while I visited the general and wanted to know how I made out. He was amazed that the general had agreed to see me. I filled him in on the details, including the coup de grâce about the general coming to the Christmas party. Within a few hours, the news was all over the job.

"Did you hear, Martin was with the general discussing a new patch?" "No, he didn't have an appointment, just walked into his office and asked to see the general." "No, the general didn't throw him out." "By the way, Martin invited him to the Christmas party, and he's going!" "That kid has some balls. We ought to make him our president." And so it went the rest of the day. Lucky for me, I was soldering up and down since my return to post, dreaming of my first organizational gain – a change in a silly patch – but still a gain.

The next week passed very quickly for me, working my duty tours and helping the other guys with the Christmas party preparations. Each guy chipped in a dollar and with 200 guys in the command, we collected $200 – a lot of money in those days. We were able to buy at least one big toy, plus a few smaller ones, for each child. We also got a lot of "goodies," such as ice cream cups, bags of candy, fruit, soda, Christmas stockings, etc., donated by businesses in the area. With their support, and the help of the staff at Roosevelt Hospital, we were able to stage a great party for the kids, and us. Santa was played by Detective Murphy, whose sparkling wit prevailed, even when one little kid tinkled on his newly purchased Santa outfit! Detective Murphy was the best Santa I have ever seen anywhere! The party was covered by *The Daily News*, *The Daily Mirror*, and *The New York Journal* and it contained pictures of the general, the captain, and me holding, or presenting, gifts to the kids. Yes, we were all friends that day and at the end of the party, I escorted the general to his car to thank him for attending. "John," he said, "I had a great time. You guys did a wonderful thing for those kids today. By the way, I spoke to the captain during the Christmas party about changing the patch. The old 'T' is out and the new patch you suggested will be issued soon. Merry Christmas, and good luck."

I replied, "Merry Christmas to you, General, and thanks." When I spread the word to the guys at the party you would have thought they had all been promoted to sergeant the way they carried on! The next month, I ran for PBA president and was elected, a job I was to be re-elected to for twelve consecutive years. That was the year that my son, Brian, was born. My cup overflowed!

Chapter 7

I was working a 4:00 p.m.-to-midnight tour the night my son was born. Eileen and I were having some coffee before I left for work, and she felt she would deliver that evening. "Maybe you ought to take the night off," she urged.

I didn't and remarked, "Don't worry, dear. You won't deliver for a few days yet." How wrong I was! I had just arrived on post and made my ring to the Operations Unit when the sergeant notified me that my wife had been rushed to the hospital to deliver a baby. I called the hospital immediately and inquired about Eileen's condition. After identifying myself to the nurse as her husband, I was informed that I was the father of a 6 lb. 8 oz. baby boy. The nurse assured me that both were doing fine and were sleeping at the moment. "Are there visiting hours this evening?" I asked. "Yes? OK, I will be there later for a quick visit. Thanks for the great news." I called the Operations Desk and requested to speak to the sergeant, who then got on the phone. "Sarge, I need a favor. My wife just had a baby and I'd like to visit her during my meal period. Is that OK with you?"

"No good, Officer," the sergeant replied. "It's not that important to let you go off post for."

"It is to me," I said, "and I'm going when my meal period arrives." And I did, grabbing the N/BA train to the 145th Street station and walking the block to the hospital. I visited Eileen first and was happy to learn that she had a much easier time delivering our son than she did delivering our daughter. She had a breech birth the first time and never quite recovered from it. Although she didn't have a breech birth this time, she still had a rough time because the baby was lodged in her tube, and this certainly complicated the birth. Eileen insisted I go see our son. I spotted his nametag on the little crib and then spent the next ten minutes studying the little guy, and maybe planning a little bit of his future at the same time. I went back and visited Eileen again, and thanked her for delivering our little boy. I promised to bring her some things she needed from home when I visited her tomorrow. I kissed her goodbye and left the hospital with a proud smile on my face, and hustled into the subway to return to my post.

When I got back on post, I fully expected to find some sergeant awaiting my return from meal. I was lucky. There was no sergeant in sight. I called back on post and spent the rest of the tour patrolling a little harder than usual to make up for my hospital visit. John, I thought, the Good Lord sure has been good to you. He's granted you twenty-eight years of life so far, took you through a depression and a World War, gave you enough brains to pass the test and get appointed to the Transit Police Department, permitted you to marry a nice girl, and then blessed you with two beautiful children. I sure had a lot to be thankful for. I was determined to pursue my newly elected PBA president's duties with increased fervor since there was much work to be done to improve the job.

You might be wondering what exactly the PBA is all about. The PBA is a line organization that represents the patrolmen. It is not, per se, a union. It is a benevolent association for the patrolmen and their families. Without the PBA, the other line organizations could not function effectively, since whatever job benefits accrue to the patrolmen are eventually granted to the other department ranks -- after the PBA has fought the good fight, many times alone. Any office held in the PBA is an elected office, and in my day, a term of office was one year. You had to be elected every year. A person in office had to be productive or else. I decided to be productive!

During my first six terms as PBA president, I received no salary from the PBA. Whatever expenses we incurred were repaid at the next PBA meeting. For those first six years, I continued my patrol assignment in District #1, working tours around the clock with rotating days off. I also worked a second job with a payroll company in the midtown area, usually two days a week. And I worked one day a week as a bartender at my partner's brother's place in Queens.

This is a good place to introduce my old partner, who is quite a guy and was one hell of a cop. His name is Jim Rooney

– James Barton Rooney, to be exact. He is from the Yorkville section of Manhattan where he learned the manly art of self-defense and became both an amateur boxer and a Golden Glover. Jim had over fifty amateur bouts, had a beautiful left hook, and was a handy guy to have around when we had to subdue some resisting felon. He was given to smoking cigars and he sure liked to take an occasional drink, which he could handle very nicely. Jim had a brother who was on the captain's list in the New York City Police Department, and his dad was a driver for the Borough President of Manhattan. My partner was about eight years older than me, making him about thirty-five at the time I first met him.

We met on patrol on a day tour and had adjoining posts. I was an "aviator" that day, which meant I had to "fly" to a post outside of my regular command. I was assigned to the 59th Street station of the Lexington Avenue subway station, which was a double post since the station contained both the IRT and IND lines. It was, therefore, a fixed post. Jimmy was assigned to cover several stations on the Lexington Avenue line and stopped off at 59th Street for his meal period. Almost all of the subway stations contain employee rooms. There are porter's rooms, maintainer's rooms, station department rooms, lighting department rooms, and crew rooms. Cops are not supposed to enter any of these rooms except for police necessity. I figured if you wanted a smoke, that was a police necessity! So I entered this particular room to grab what I thought would be a quick smoke. It was the beginning of a partnership that lasted over twelve years, for Jim was already in the room when I came in. We hit it off immediately, talking about what had to be done to improve the job, and how to go about doing it. Jim would leave the 59th Street station, check the rest of his post, and return to 59th Street to talk some more. By the end of that tour, we were old buddies, about to launch an attack against the "Old Order." We met several times after that first meeting, and finally hit upon a plan to secure leadership of the PBA. I was, at that time, already serving as the 2nd vice president, and in winning the battle of the "patch," I had a good following of PBA voters. We wanted to develop a team concept in running for office, so we came up with a slate just like politicians do. And Jim was a politician! We decided on the following campaign slogan:

VOTE THE RAM
Rooney for Vice President
Atkins for 2nd Vice President
Martin for President

We had a drawing made up of a RAM battering the door to our headquarters building seeking the following goals:
- Unlimited Sick Leave
- 27 Days Vacation
- Improved Work Chart
- Salary Increase
- 20-Year, ½ Pay Retirement Plan

The posters were distributed throughout the job and our entire slate was elected to PBA office.

In the ensuing twelve years, we would accomplish all the goals stated on our first campaign poster, plus many, many other gains. None of these accomplishments was easy. Most of them required long, hard-fought efforts before they were obtained. Much too much of the burden of raising our children fell upon my wife, Eileen. Too many times she had to go to family gatherings without me because I would be involved in PBA matters. On at least three occasions, after being hospitalized for health reasons, she had to get some friend or relative to drive her home from the hospital because something came up with the PBA that I had to handle personally. It was really rough on her, and I'll never be able to make up those years. During those years, it seems that I placed the job ahead of Eileen and the kids. I didn't mean to do it; it just happened that way. I rationalized that I was doing it for them really, for by improving the job, I was improving their lifestyle. That is partly true, but was it worth the time we could have spent together? I must admit, that during my PBA tenure, things were very interesting and exciting for me. We met people from all walks of life including governors, lieutenant governors, the attorney general, members of the State legislature, members of the United States Congress, members of city government, and police officers from all over the State of New York.

The greatest guy Jim and I ever met, and worked with for many years, was Robert F. Wagner, the mayor of the

City of New York. All of the benefits we obtained for our members were granted by Bob Wagner. Not right away, of course. The mayor liked to take his time deliberating about the issues, but in the end, he always came through for us. He never once refused to meet with us when he was asked – and we asked often! It was certainly amazing that with all the problems the mayor had on his mind, he would always find time to help us with ours. It was an understood fact around City Hall that Martin and Rooney had an open invitation to contact the mayor on almost a daily basis. The "Palace Guard" never stopped us from approaching the mayor as he was either walking up, or down, the steps at City Hall – a favorite tactic of ours. In fact, many times, the Palace Guard would provide us with a copy of the mayor's daily schedule so that we could setup our ambush at other locations if we missed him at City Hall. Bob Wagner never seemed to mind where we popped up. I think he regarded us as his good luck charms. He called us "The Gold Dust Twins," but he was always the one that delivered the "pot of gold." He seemed to enjoy our contrasting styles of operating. We were always trying to climb the biggest mountains in seeking to obtain benefits that would put the transit police on a par with our counterparts in the New York City Police Department. A near impossible task at the time, but we did it eventually, thanks to the mayor's solid support. Let me now tell you how and why.

Chapter 8

First of all, we came up with the word **Parity**. Parity is defined in Webster's Dictionary as "the quality of being equal." We felt that we in the transit police had equal job duties, and faced the same risks, as the city police. We had to take similar examinations; we wore identical uniforms (*except for the patch*); and enforced the same laws. Why shouldn't we receive the same job benefits? It was very difficult to convince the elected officials of that fact, however. Don't forget, the city police had been in business for at least 100 years and was the largest police force in the entire country, if not in the entire world. And here we come, from the subway yet, requesting (*we never demanded – we couldn't afford to*) parity with them!

At first, we were rebuffed with sardonic comments by those who refused to take an objective view of our position. They thought we would simply fade back into the subways and never surface again. Or that maybe we would drown in a sea of fresh air if permitted to walk a beat on the city's streets. We just continued to pursue our parity goal, chipping away day after day, week after week, month after month, year after year – relentlessly, gaining new benefits each year and closing the parity gap. After twelve years of effort, we had just about obtained parity with the New York City Police Department. Again, I want to state emphatically that TOTAL PARITY would not have been possible without the enduring help and approval of Mayor Robert F. Wagner. He helped make two transit cops, known as the Gold Dust Twins, look good!

I think I should relate just a few of the situations we went through in gaining parity with the New York City Police Department. First, there was a time when we were pushing very hard for a twenty-year, half-pay retirement plan for our members. We had gone through all of the preliminary steps – drafting the necessary legislation; getting both a state senator and a state assemblyman to introduce the bill in the state legislature; getting the City Council to sponsor a Home Rule Message; lobbied in Albany for four months to get the bill out of committee, and voted on favorably; spoke to the lieutenant governor and all members of the legislature. We were now in the final assault stages and required the approval of the mayor. He was, unfortunately, particularly busy at the time and all efforts to get that one, crucial meeting had met with negative results – in spite of our "haunting" the steps of City Hall. The mayor just couldn't spare the time to see us. Our spirits sank lower and lower and Jim and I took turns bolstering each other's morale. We had to hang in there or we would fail, and that was something neither of us was willing to accept. Every day, the mayor would have to pass us on the steps of City Hall and he would always have a word of encouragement for us. "I'm trying to get the time to have that meeting with you boys. I know you won't go away until I do."

We were down to the last week of the legislative session and this was our seventh attempt (a seven-year effort!) at the "20" bill. Jim and I had pulled on a lot of coattails during those years, and had left our families alone many, many times while knocking ourselves out on that bill. We just couldn't bear to lose now that we were so close. It was the final, and biggest, barrier to full parity and full police acceptance. So, our vigil continued on the steps at City Hall. Late one afternoon during that final week, the mayor passed us on the steps and noticed that Jim and I were giving him "the ice cubes" by staring coldly at him. He stopped in his tracks and asked, "Boys, would you like to take a ride with me in my limousine up to Gracie Mansion? We can solve the pension problem on the way uptown. What with the rush hour traffic and all, you guys will have ample time to convince me to approve the pension bill." You should have seen our faces when Mayor Wagner invited us for that ride! We were like two little kids in a candy factory. We both tried to appear nonchalant, saying, "OK, Mayor. We don't mind taking a car ride." We almost tripped over each other getting into the mayor's limousine. I sat in the back seat, next to the mayor, hoping to get his good ear (he was slightly deaf in one ear). And Jim was fumbling with the jump seat, finally crunching his ever-present cigar in the seat in his eagerness to get in. Eventually, we regained our composure, the detective bodyguard closed the door, and the mayor's car turned out of City Hall into the evening rush hour traffic. We never noticed it! The trip took maybe twenty-five minutes during which we bombarded the mayor with reasons why he should approve our twenty-year pension bill. By the time we arrived at Gracie Mansion, the mayor had agreed to approve it. The following week, the bill was passed and the next month was signed into law by Governor Rockefeller, who was urged to sign it by Lieutenant Governor Malcolm Wilson. The year was 1964 – a very good year for the Transit Police Department.

Just to step back a moment, a year or so before the mayor approved the pension plan, we got involved in an effort to get the City of New York to consolidate the transit police into the City Police Department, since consolidation would certainly facilitate gaining parity between the two police forces. I should point out that from the very first day we were on the job, we heard rumors about consolidation. In all my thirty-plus years on the job, there must have been at least a dozen studies or surveys regarding consolidation. Every time a survey was conducted by non-police people, consolidation was always strongly recommended. It was a pure and simple business matter – it would reduce, or remove, duplication of effort; unify control and command; save the taxpayers millions of dollars; and would be in the public interest. Every time such a survey was conducted by

police personnel, either city police or transit police, consolidation was never recommended. These consolidation
efforts always created tension and ill-feeling between the
two forces. Such ill-feeling usually disappeared after a few
weeks, probably because we both realized that we needed
each other. It seems the "troops" in our department favored
the merger, and the big bosses wanted no part of it. It was
during the last, and biggest, consolidation effort, in my last
year of service as PBA president that things really started to
heat up.

Jim and I were now first grade detectives – in spite of
the fact that we couldn't find the American flag in a phone
booth! We had advanced to that grade by virtue of our PBA
efforts since one of our accomplishments included the creation of a detective division. We certainly felt we deserved
to be first grade detectives – we worked hard to establish
the detective division, and had sadly neglected our own
families in doing it. At least as first graders, we earned additional pay for our families. Even if we were no "Sherlock
Holmes," we could still make "collars," when we could find
the time. At least we both looked the part – with our Ivy
League suits, candy striped ties, brown shoes, and Frank
Sinatra type fedoras! That year, we again approached Mayor
Wagner, proposing consolidation as a way of his granting us
a twenty-year pension without opening the door to other
city uniform groups who would be seeking such a benefit
now that the mayor "broke the sound barrier" by granting
us the pension plan. The mayor agreed to refer the matter to

the city police commissioner. We were not happy with the mayor's plan and we told him so. "Mr. Mayor," I said, "the Police Commissioner will zap us."

"He won't zap you," Mayor Wagner replied. "He's a good fellow." Since the mayor had made up his mind, we had to go along with his plan. We decided to mount an offensive through some newspaper friends, and at least try to charm the police commissioner into seeing our side of the picture.

What a case! The police commissioner at the time was a gentleman who had many years of police experience. He had been a state trooper before joining the New York City Police Department and he became the youngest sergeant promoted to that rank in the City Police Department. He advanced rapidly through the ranks all the way up to chief inspector, before he was appointed police commissioner. In addition, he had earned a law degree and was a member of the New York State Bar. He was an extremely qualified and tough adversary! Undaunted, we set out to convince him of the wisdom of consolidation. We had learned that the police commissioner frequently ate lunch in a restaurant on Park Row, so we decided to eat our lunch there regularly. We became friendly with the restaurant owner who somehow got the impression that Jim and I were two of the police commissioner's favorite detectives.

It didn't take us too long to locate the table where the commissioner sat, after which we always grabbed a table nearby. This way, we would have a chance to say hello and just maybe be able to use the occasion to win him over to our side. It had the opposite effect! One day the owner, thinking that the police commissioner would not show, gave us his table. We were halfway through our lunch when in walked the police commissioner with an entourage of high-level brass! He was flabbergasted, red-faced, irate, and I think amused – all at the same time. We both jumped up and immediately offered him his favorite table, which he refused to accept. "Thank you, fellas, but no. Enjoy your lunch. We'll get another table." As he headed for another table, he whispered to me, "John, you'd better not hope for consolidation. If it happens, your assignments won't be too good." As we passed his table later on while leaving, he called us over to his table and introduced us to his top staff. In parting, he added good-naturedly, "these are the two guys who are giving us that consolidation." We countered that if consolidation did happen, we'd see that all of them kept their positions! We all had a good laugh and parted friends.

Jim and I never sat at the police commissioner's table again. In fact, we were lucky the owner let us sit any place in the restaurant again! Shortly after the "restaurant incident," I was granted a meeting with the police commissioner to review the results of his consolidation survey. I was nervous as I entered the old police headquarters building at 240 Centre Street and walked up the one flight of stairs to the commissioner's office. It was the very same office that Teddy Roosevelt occupied when he served as police commissioner.

I introduced myself to the sergeant outside the commissioner's office, adding that I had an appointment. "Go right in, John, the commissioner is waiting for you." As I entered, I remembered a line from the Charge of the Light Brigade, "into the valley of death rode the six hundred." Where were the other 599?

The police commissioner was sitting at his desk and he stood up when I entered, shook hands, offered me a seat, and rang for coffee for the both of us. No one else was in the room as we leisurely drank our coffee and got set to square off on the consolidation issue. At least the police commissioner had class – he didn't just rush into the bad news and show me the door. He appreciated the tremendous effort we had put into the matter and respected us for it. Unfortunately, his survey and study did not recommend consolidation. I told him I expected that would be the result of such a police survey and that I had told the mayor that would be the result from the very beginning. "Would you mind telling me why your department is against consolidation, Commissioner?" I asked.

He replied, "John, the report is about six inches thick, but off the top of my head…" He went on to enumerate some of the reasons and this prompted a twenty-minute debate between us that got me absolutely nowhere. The meeting ended with him advising me to go back to City Hall to haunt the mayor. "He's the one with the power to do it if he really wants the headache." We shook hands and I left, my last recollection of the police commissioner being that he shook his head while smiling sadly. He looked relieved!

Back I went to City Hall to haunt the mayor, again feeling hopeless and unhappy at the thought of reporting the bad news to the membership. Mayor Wagner saw me immediately. "I told you in the beginning that the police department would zap us, Mr. Mayor." "John," said the mayor, "sit down and listen. There are just too many difficulties to overcome relative to consolidation at this time for me to override their recommendations. You fellas fought hard and tried to make it easier for me to get your people the twenty-year pension through consolidation. We just can't do it at this time. I promise you – next year you'll have the twenty-year pension."

That was good enough for me. True to his word, the next year Mayor Wagner granted a twenty-year retirement plan to the transit police. Although full consolidation still hadn't happened, it was getting closer.

Chapter 9

During my twelve years as PBA President, Jim and I managed to obtain many benefits for our members. Sometimes, the things we fought for should have been routine decisions made by management. For example, it is clearly management's responsibility to provide the necessary tools and equipment required to get the job accomplished. Things like radio cars and sufficient manpower rightfully fall into that category. Our big bosses hardly ever pushed for such items. It fell upon the PBA's shoulders to seek these items, or suffer in silence without them. We decided to push. I'll never forget the cynical comments made by some of the bosses the first time we proposed the use of patrol cars for the transit police. "How are you going to get these cars into the subway?" "Will they run on the tracks?" Naturally we didn't propose to run these radio cars in the subways! They were to be used to supplement the foot patrol officers, providing them with a method of fast response to police conditions. Without the radio cars, the transit police officers had to wait for the next subway train in order to respond to a police condition which could have occurred say two stations away – some twenty blocks. At certain times, the headway, or waiting time, between trains was almost thirty minutes. Imagine having to wait that long in order to respond to a violent crime in progress? After a public campaign, again aided by the help of some of our newspaper friends, we successfully convinced the big bosses of the necessity of using radio cars as a legitimate police tool. Once we obtained these vehicles, they became a favorite of those very cynics who initially opposed their use – and then they took full credit for the idea! Oh well, what else is new?

As for the question of adequate manpower, these same big bosses were again very reluctant to press for any increase, leaving the pushing to the PBA. We didn't hesitate to pick up the gauntlet and started our usual newspaper campaign. The headlines read, "WILD WEST RIDES THE SUBWAYS," "MURDER ON A TRAIN," and "RAPE AT HIGH NOON ON THE SUBWAY." Within a short period of time, the transit police force was increased from 500 to 1,000 members, thereby providing the riding public with vastly improved police protection. Taking on such initiatives never made me popular with the big bosses, but I sure made a hit with the troops in the trenches, and it really helped the public get improved service from the transit police.

During my tenure as Transit Police PBA president, I also became very active on a State Police Conference level.

The State Police Conference, at the time, was an organization that represented over 500 separate police departments throughout the state and over 50,000 civil service police officers. It took our outfit a few years to be accepted as conference members. Once accepted, we really became active in that organization, serving initially on any committee assignments farmed out to us. After a short period of time, I decided to seek state office. The board of officers nominated me for vice president at the annual state convention held at Grossinger's in the Catskill Mountains. That year, the incumbent president and vice president were supposed to be shoo-ins for reelection. But that was until the transit police got into the act! What was supposed to be a quick, half-hour, orderly election turned into a heated, six hour parliamentary slugfest that ended in a "Mexican standoff." When the smoke finally cleared, a compromise president was selected, and I managed to get elected state vice president. The transit police had arrived on the state scene! I served two years as state vice president and then ran for president, only to be defeated the first time. The gentleman that won the president's job that year was a highly qualified police officer from a small department just outside of Buffalo. He did a fine job as president that year, but the next year, we faced off again. This time, I won election by a mere three votes. We had waged a very political-type campaign for the presidency, complete with posters. The posters had a picture of me in uniform with the following captions:

Alarm #666 [my shield number] -- This man is wanted –
To improve the lot of ALL policemen in the State.
Have gun will travel to obtain decent salaries and
improved working conditions for all police officers.

The posters really helped to get me elected. Now I had to prove I could deliver, which I did because I had a good product to sell – cops! It was a great personal honor being elected president of the State Police Conference, and it was also an honor for the Transit Police Department. It marked the first time a state president was elected from other than a city, town, village, or county police force. It was the very first time that an agency or authority police force member had been elected to lead the 50,000 police officers throughout the State of New York. I served two terms as state president and then stepped down -- I felt that such an honor should be afforded to other qualified people -- and the conference had so many qualified candidates. Besides, my family was again being neglected by all my activities. It was definitely time to step down. I will always be grateful for the honor and privilege of serving, the experience gained, and the many fine people I met along the way.

Since the PBA years are at an end, I think it appropriate to list and perhaps offer a few brief comments on those people I remember as being very much a part of it. I will probably not remember all of them because there are so many and of course, memory grows dimmer with the passing years. Any omissions will not be intended and I hope forgiven. So, here we go.

You already know the major role played by my pal and old partner, Detective James Rooney, so no further comment on Jim is necessary.

The same goes for Mayor Bob Wagner. Let it suffice to say, "He was the Greatest."

I mentioned Governor Rockefeller briefly as signing into law the twenty-year pension bill. He also signed four other bills into law for us – two as Transit Police president and two as State Police Conference president. He always attended the state conference conventions and was in our corner all the way. He was truly a good guy and a great governor.

Malcolm Wilson, lieutenant governor, was a terrific guy, an accomplished orator, an exceptional legislator, a true friend, and a solid supporter. His door was always open, and he always found the time to help. He should have been elected governor (Damn that stupid Watergate incident – it sure hurt the chances of so many fine Republicans who had nothing to do with it.)

Special mention must be made of Thomas J. Mackell. Tom was a former detective in the New York City Police Department who left the department to go into private law practice after passing the bar examinations. He was elected a state senator and served several terms as a member of the state legislature. It was while in that capacity that Jim and I first met the senator. We were driving up to Albany in Jim's car, a black sedan that looked exactly like a detective squad car which, of course, was no accident. We had stopped momentarily to make sure we were taking the right road to Albany. Just then, a car pulled alongside and a very distinguished gentleman, with a big Irish face and a head of wavy gray hair, leaned out of the car window. He inquired if we were a couple of the boys from New York, meaning the New York City Police Department. We beamed and replied, "Detectives Martin and Rooney from the transit police. We are on our way to Albany to meet Senator Tom Mackell."

The gray-haired guy laughed and said, "I'm Tom Mackell, follow us." When we got to Albany, the senator and his aide, "Bunky," got us a room in their hotel; gave us the senator's office and hotel numbers; provided us with a listing of all the legislators; gave us a briefing on how the legislature functioned; introduced us to whatever legislators were around the hotel; and generally got us started on the legislative scene. From that day on, Tom Mackell was our constant friend, advisor, and sponsor of all our bills (several of which he had passed and enacted into law). He was most respected and liked on "the hill," for not only was he a dedicated legislator, but a terrific singer with a marvelous tenor voice. Tom didn't just sing Irish songs. He sang all kinds of songs in several languages. His version of "My Yiddishe Mama" was a show stopper, and a vote-getter. Tom had German songs, Italian songs, Polish songs, French songs, Greek songs – you name it, he sang it, and he sang them all well.

Naturally, the senator was very popular, not only in

Albany, but just about everywhere he went. Tom taught us the ropes well and in a short time, Jim and I became accomplished lobbyists and well known on "the hill." We were by this time, "professional haunters," and quite proficient at shaking hands, grabbing coattails, ringing doorbells, etc. We certainly were not bashful and could cite our own causes with ease. We did well in Albany! But without Senator Tom Mackell, it never would have happened. The senator later went on to become the district attorney of Queens County. I will never forget Tom and all that he did. What a guy!

New York City Transit Authority commissioners Charlie Patterson, Joe O'Grady, Vince Curtayne, Dan Scannell, Jack Gilhooley, and General Casey -- all solid guys whose understanding, and cooperation, helped us advance the transit police force to the professional reputation it enjoys today. Without their help, transit cops might well still be "specials," dressed in drab gray uniforms.

Frank Prial II, editor of the leading Civil Service newspaper, *The Chief,* and our PBA attorney for all twelve years that I was PBA president. Frank was with us from the beginning. We went to see him in his office right after we were elected PBA officers and we hit it off right away. He agreed to represent us legally and to make full use of the voice of his mighty Civil Service newspaper – a newspaper held in high esteem by all government officials in the State of New York. Frank's grandfather had founded the paper before the turn of the century and many a politician felt the sting of that paper's arrows. *The Chief* called them as they saw them.

Despite the fact that Frank came from an entirely different background than Jim and I, we got along extremely well and worked together to accomplish our goals. Frank was at his best as a mediator – he could really separate the "chaff from the wheat" at the bargaining table. His quiet, reserved, gentlemanly manner was dynamite. As Jim would say, "Frank could really handle himself in the clinches."

A couple of Frank's top editors, Charlie Liebman and Dick Bodenheimer, also deserve mention. Both of these guys were of enormous help, writing the stories, contacting officials, and doing a lot of the research behind the scene. They did their jobs well and deserve a special "thank you."

Next are the guys in the trenches – the guys on the job and in the PBA who, day in and day out, and without the fanfare and recognition Jim and I received, did a great job. The Roll Call of Honor includes:

Johnny Atkins, 2nd vice president, PBA.

Johnny Nove, 2nd vice president, PBA.

Ed Collins, secretary, PBA.

Ed was a lieutenant, a former sailor off the USS Dakota, a special advisor to me when we patrolled our posts as cops, and a very special friend. Rest in Peace, Ed – you earned it.

Lou Staudenbaur, retired detective and former delegate-at-large, PBA. Known as "Lefty Louie," he and Ed Collins campaigned all over the State of New York to get me elected state president. They spoke to just about every PBA president in the state, extolling my good points. They did a great job and got me elected. Both of them were tireless workers and deserve much recognition for a job well done. They certainly belong in the PBA Hall of Fame.

Julie Aschendorf, 2nd vice president, PBA and a retired police officer after thirty-five years of service. Julie is another ex-sailor, a former chief petty officer in the Navy. He did so many things well, a real switch hitter who could handle any job assigned to him. Enjoy your retirement years, Chief.

Al Sgaglione, State Police Conference President. I first met Al when he was a newly elected PBA President of the Port Authority of New York Police and I was the newly elected PBA President of the transit police. We started our PBA service around the same time. Al served as my secretary and treasurer of the State Conference when I was president. We learned a lot together. Al used to joke with me about not pushing me out of office, but when I stepped down, would I endorse him – and I did exactly that.

"Broadway Bob" Gordon, vice president, New York State Police Conference. Bob was the most dapper cop in the whole state and was an extremely hard worker. He retired as a detective in the Freeport Police Department and went on to become an officer in the National Police Organization.

US Congressman Mario Biaggi, a former lieutenant in the New York City Police Department and that department's most decorated police officer. He was always a friend and a most able legislator.

Chief Thomas J. O'Rourke, former chief, New York City Transit Police and the first chief appointed from our ranks. Chief O'Rourke was a former lieutenant commander, US

Navy, assigned to naval intelligence, and was the best chief any police department could have had. He was also one of the youngest to be so appointed.

All of our deputy chiefs, assistant chiefs, deputy assistant chiefs, inspectors, deputy inspectors, captains, lieutenants, sergeants, detectives, and last, but most important, the police officers. They all helped in making the Transit Police Department the fine department it is today.

Those members of the Federal Bureau of Investigation whose professional assistance and early recognition of the Transit Police Department was most welcome and appreciated.

Chapter 10

My service as PBA president ended in November 1965, the very year that the Transit Police Department exploded in size from 1,000 members to over 3,000 members – a 300% increase, making it the second largest police force in the state and the sixth largest police force in the entire country. This tremendous increase was brought about as a result of a series of violent crimes, including two shocking homicides that occurred on moving subway trains.

One of the homicides took place when an off-duty, first grade detective from the New York City Police Department was held up on a Brooklyn IRT subway train in the Flatbush Avenue Station only two days before Christmas. Three culprits surprised the off-duty officer by drawing guns and demanding his money. The officer responded by drawing his revolver and identifying himself as a police officer. Before he could fire, he was cut down in a hail of bullets. The officer still managed to get off some shots, wounding one of the perpetrators before he succumbed to his wounds. Detective Steve O'Connor of the Transit Police Department was on bus patrol on the street, heard the gunfire, and observed three suspects fleeing on foot and heading west on Flatbush Avenue. Detective O'Connor commandeered a passing car and pursued and captured two of the culprits. The other culprit was nabbed by two city cops responding to the condition in a radio patrol car. This was a classic example of coordination and cooperation between two separate police departments in real live street action. The officers returned to the subway station with the suspects where they were positively identified by several witnesses to the shooting.

The second homicide took place in Brooklyn and involved a seventeen-year old youth who was riding home on the subway at about 10:30 p.m. The youth was returning to his home after visiting his girlfriend in Queens. He was approached by three other youths who demanded money and a cigarette. One of the youths held a bayonet in his hand and when the youth being accosted said he had no cigarettes because he didn't smoke, the youth with the bayonet plunged into the boy's throat and back. The culprits then fled the train at the next station, leaving their victim slumped on the subway train floor where he bled to death. What a waste of a good boy's life at the hands of senseless assassins! My partner, along with several detectives from the transit police, was assigned to work on the case. The case turned out to be another classic example of coordination between two separate police forces working together to solve a particularly violent and shocking crime. Our boss and squad commander, Lieutenant "Mac," a real sharp detective, worked out the detective assignments and stakeouts with the city police squad commander in the precinct concerned. It was decided that the detective teams assigned would consist of one city detective and one transit detective so that each detective could better utilize and share his particular expertise. Since part of the investigation would involve street and subway areas, the detectives familiarized themselves with both. It was good planning and a brand new technique that paid off with the eventual arrest and convictions of the three culprits. Thanks to Lieutenant Mac's plan, new rapport and mutual respect between the two departments' detective divisions ensued. The lieutenant's tactic is still used today and is still getting the same productive results.

Both of these shocking murders received tremendous media coverage. The public outcry directly resulted in the huge increase in the size of the Transit Police Department and proved that ensuring the safety of the public is a top priority, even in light of budget constraints. Naturally, it took time to recruit, conduct the necessary civil service examinations, publish an eligible list, investigate the candidates, and make appointments. They had to undergo training at the Police Academy for at least twelve weeks, and this tremendous task was assigned to Deputy Inspector Charlie "G," his executive officer, Lieutenant Charlie "D," and another officer, Lieutenant "F." At the time, the Transit Police Academy was located in a National Guard Armory on Main Street in Flushing, Queens. Our department had obtained use of the armory through the efforts of Deputy Inspector G who just happened to be a lieutenant colonel in the Army Reserve. The building was suitable for normal training needs, but was not large enough to adequately process the large recruit classes being trained. Lieutenant D and Lieutenant F were assigned the task of locating additional training facilities. They did their job well and within a few days, came up with two additional armories. The department was now prepared to train over 2,000 new police officers. Most of these new officers were very young, the average age being about twenty-three. However, many of them were mature beyond their years since most of them served in the armed forces during the Vietnam War. These guys were really good and soon were making their presence felt in the transit system. The public loved them! And once again, the subways belonged to the riding public and not the bad guys.

Once the new recruits were out of the Police Academy and assigned to patrol duties, subway felony crime decreased by a startling 62%! The Transit Police Department did not accomplish this remarkable decrease solely by themselves. We had solid, professional help from the New York City Police Department who were directed by Mayor Wagner to assign 600 city cops on the subway system every night during the hours of 8:00 p.m. to 4:00 a.m. The transit police were also directed by the mayor to assign 600 transit cops during those same hours, for a combined total of 1,200 officers. With such a huge deployment of manpower, every train and every station was covered by at least one police officer. The subways became the safest place in the Big Apple!

As a result of these increased, inter-departmental police assignments, the general public and the riding public benefited – because both elements of the population learned very quickly that the quickest and surest way to get police assistance during the night hours was by entering any subway station. It became commonplace for a police officer on subway duty to become involved in police conditions that were initiated on the city's streets. Many outstanding arrests involving street crimes were made as a result. I recall one incident in which a transit police officer on patrol of an elevated subway station in Queens observed a burglary in progress in a store on the street below. The officer waited until the burglar's truck was fully loaded with television sets, and then radioed the condition to the operations unit. The operations unit in turn requested assistance from the appropriate city precinct and the officer subsequently went down to the street and apprehended the criminals. There were similar collars made through elevated patrol observations of crimes in progress on the streets below. So it's clear that not only the riding public, but also the general public, received better police protection as a result of Mayor Wagner's program.

Placing a police officer on every train and in every station during select hours was a very good tactic at the time. However, as with all good plans, flaws can develop in the plan that require administrators to remain flexible and make adjustments as dictated by the circumstances -- be ready to redeploy manpower to other time slots in order to better cope with emerging crime patterns and conditions. Unfortunately, the department remained locked in and committed to deploying the 1,200 officers throughout the subway system only during 8:00 p.m. to 4:00 a.m. hours. It should be noted that every station is different, meaning that they are not the same size nor are the type and volume of crime committed. All of the stations should have been weighted according to crime statistics, passenger volume, geographical area, and primary purpose of the area being served by the subway (e.g., business, recreational, residential). Certain stations are very busy and have a high incidence of repeating crimes, and these might require as many as four officers. While other less active stations may not require even one officer for an entire tour. Such low activity stations could have patrol presence provided by a foot officer covering two or more such stations, further supported by special attention from the sector patrol car. It makes no sense to arbitrarily assign the same number of officers to each station. The "bad guys" size up the static picture after a while and merely shift their criminal activities into other hours when the police presence is far less. And that is exactly what happened to the Transit Police Enforcement Program. Crime shifted to other hours while the troops were still deployed in large numbers to the 8:00 p.m. to 4:00 a.m. time frame. Eventually, the condition was corrected and manpower was redeployed to other hours with very effective results (more about that later).

Chapter 11

As I mentioned in the previous chapter, my PBA activities, including my State Police Conference duties, ended in 1965. In fact, they ended rather abruptly. Why? For a good reason actually – I was promoted to sergeant. Since the PBA was an association that served the patrolmen, I could no longer be part of that group. So, there I was, after fifteen years serving with the troops in the trenches, starting a new career as a boss! A view from the other side, so to speak, and it felt very uncomfortable to me. After all those years representing and fighting for the men – the police officers and detectives – that do the job at the gut level of execution, now I was a part of management. I did a lot of soul searching and finally concluded that I could still help the troops in so many ways without compromising my role as a supervisor. I resolved to be a fair leader who could show compassion and relate, when and where needed, in order to inspire the men to get the job done more effectively.

Making sergeant initially did not bring too much joy into the Martin household, mainly because it resulted in a loss in pay of about $4,500 – a lot of money back in those days. Some promotion! How can a person get promoted and suffer such a heavy cut in pay? Here's why. During my final years as PBA president, I received a stipend of $1,800 per year while so serving. By then, I was also a first grade detective and first grade detectives received the same salary as a lieutenant. So the difference in pay scale between sergeant and lieutenant, combined with the loss of the PBA stipend, came to about $4,500. Naturally, my wife Eileen wasn't thrilled. Who would be? We really couldn't afford the loss of income at the time – my daughter, Susan, was in her first year of college and my son, Brian, had just begun his first year at Archbishop Molloy High School. It was really rough for a while and we argued frequently about the merits of my making sergeant.

"What's the big deal about being a sergeant?" Eileen would ask. "Do you like to wear stripes on your arm while we can't pay the kids school bills?"

I would answer, "Eileen, sergeant is a permanent civil service rank. A detective is a patrolman detailed to serve as a detective and that detail can be revoked at any time without cause. It is not a civil service protected position. Besides, I can't make lieutenant and captain without becoming a sergeant first."

"I hope it doesn't take you another fifteen years to make lieutenant," she said.

"Stick with me, kid and I'll have you on Broadway yet," I answered. And so the discussion went, day after day, and usually when we were eating. It certainly didn't help make the food taste better, and it didn't do the digestive tract any good either. Of course, I couldn't blame her for being upset about the loss of all that pay. In addition, they put me back working tours around the clock, including weekends! I didn't smile too much for a while as a new sergeant until my old partner, Jim Rooney, went to bat for me. Jim had succeeded me as PBA president when I was promoted to sergeant, filling my unexpired term. He contacted the three Transit Authority commissioners, Joe O'Grady, Dan Scannell, and Jack Gilhooley, informing them of my plight. They were amazed to learn that "my promotion" had cost my family a loss of $4,500 income per year and agreed with my wife's feelings. "How can we correct the problem for John?" they asked.

"Well, Commissioners," said Jim, "if you make John a detective sergeant, he would pick up the money he lost." He added, "There just happens to be such an opening in the Detective Division right now. After all, John was a detective for six years and can do the job easily." The commissioners took care of the matter that very day by appointing me a detective sergeant. In addition, they adopted a resolution making it retroactive to the date of my promotion to patrol sergeant, thus restoring all lost monies! The commissioners noted that I had done so much for the job and had always been fair and reasonable with them over the years. They felt I deserved a reward, and not a penalty, for being promoted. What swell guys, and what a great ex-partner!! All was normal again in the Martin household!

I settled down in my new assignment, secure in the knowledge that although I didn't get a monetary raise for making sergeant, at least I didn't lose money over it. I decided to study hard and began attending classes at Delehanty's Institute, taking a Police Academy Supervisory course. I also enrolled at John Jay College of Criminal Justice. I was determined to make captain, for that was the only way I could increase the pay I had been receiving as a first grade detective and serving as PBA president. I wanted Eileen to see that making sergeant really was a good move.

I had set a tough goal for myself, but what could I lose by trying? These civil service examinations are a lot like a lottery. So many hundreds of qualified police officers compete for a very small number of vacant positions at a higher rank. So, you pay your money and take your chances, paying your tuition, going to school, and studying at home or on the train en route to work. Your social life, which was zilch to begin with due to the rotating tours, grinds to a screeching halt as you try to absorb all the study material they throw at you. I figured I spent an average of six hours a day on home study alone when I was preparing for these examinations. The odds of being promoted were certainly stacked against you. Consider the fact that our department had a force of 3,600 members and the quota of captains was only 36 – one out of every 100 police officers can make captain – rough odds in any profession. The classroom sessions at Delehanty's were always very informative, interesting, and thanks to one man, very entertaining. Henry Mulhearn, a retired captain from the New York City Police Department, was our teacher. Captain Mulhearn was also a former New York City schoolteacher and he had a talent and a flair for teaching that was second to none. I don't know what Delehanty's paid him, but I'll tell you this – it wasn't enough. There are high-ranking police officers in just about every police department in the metropolitan area who owe a great part of their career success to Henry Mulhearn. I know I do! I still call on him from time to time for advice, and he always comes up with the right answers.

Luckily for me, it didn't take me fifteen years to make lieutenant as Eileen feared. I was very fortunate to make lieutenant approximately one year after being promoted to sergeant. Once again, by being promoted, I lost my detail as a detective sergeant supervisor and was reassigned to the patrol division. It was back to the routine of around-the-clock tours and working weekends. I think Eileen was beginning to believe that maybe, just maybe, I'd make captain yet – without it taking another fifteen years! I enjoyed being a lieutenant. It was a comfortable link in the chain of command. The sergeants did a lot of the paperwork, including the patrol and response work, as directed by the lieutenants. The captains had overall responsibility for a command, including the many problems that come along in an active command. The lieutenants were somewhere in the middle – in this case, "the middle" was the best spot. A lieutenant's role in our department has since changed and the lieutenants now bear a heavy responsibility as desk officers. I served as a lieutenant when the "lifestyle" was a lot less demanding.

After about three years of patrol lieutenant duty, I was placed in charge of the Department's Firearms Training Unit. It was an assignment I greatly enjoyed, giving me the opportunity to teach – not only recruits, but all department members, from the commissioners and chief right on down.

Department policy required all members of the force to qualify at the pistol range three times a year. During my time of service as a range officer, we were still using the old department methods of firearms qualification. This meant firing a total of thirty rounds of department-issued, 158 grain, .38 caliber ammunition in the following order:

- Ten rounds – SLOW FIRE – no time limit
- Ten rounds – TIMED FIRE – five rounds each twenty seconds, twice
- Ten rounds – RAPID FIRE – five rounds each ten seconds, twice

All firing was done at a distance of sixty feet at standard, Army "L" Bull's Eye paper targets. Scored ratings were as follows:

- 100 to 95 = EXPERT
- 94 to 85 = SHARPSHOOTER
- 84 to 75 = MARKSMAN

An expert shooter could earn up to 6 additional days off

per year provided he obtained a total score of 265 or better out of a possible 300. Such incentives motivated many of the members to improve their shooting ability. An average of 12% of the force managed to qualify as experts; about 25% qualified as sharpshooters and earned an additional three days off per year; and about 40% qualified as marksman, earning no additional days off. The remaining 23% were happy just to obtain the minimum qualifying scores. I guess it's like golf – some break eighty, some break ninety, and some are happy shooting 110.

In order to generate more shooting interest by the members of the force, I proposed an entirely different type of shooting concept, a concept that had been tried, proven and accepted by the FBI and other police departments. It was called the *Combat Pistol Course* and basically involved shooting at silhouette targets. All firing was "double action" at varying distances and under unexpected circumstances, much like at officer would encounter while on actual patrol. None of that "cock and aim, watch your front and rear sights, squeeze the trigger" jazz! Strictly, point, fire-lock your hands and arms, and shoot – just like it would be under actual street combat conditions. I should note at this point that police shooting statistics indicate that in most gun fire exchanges, the distance involved is about eight feet. Therefore, it was obvious that we should adapt our firearms training program to match realistic street and subway conditions. I submitted several reports on the subject which resulted in the department adopting the *Combat Course*.

It began to get positive results almost immediately as our officers in the field became involved in several real-life shooting incidents. It was the responsibility of the Firearms Unit to review and interview the officers and the circumstances of each shooting incident. We were pleased to learn that the Combat Course firearms training was a major factor in saving many of the officers' lives. We experienced very few situations in which an innocent bystander was hit by an officer's gunfire. In fact, there was only one such incident, a tragic situation that involved a nineteen-year old woman. A plainclothes officer on anti-crime patrol in the 34th Street station of the BMT subway observed a young male jump over the turnstile to avoid payment of the $.50 fare. The officer's order for the petty thief to stop was ignored and the young culprit kept running toward the subway train platform. The pursuing officer caught up with him on the crowded subway platform, where a violent struggle ensued. The culprit drew a knife and slashed the officer several times, forcing the officer to draw his revolver, which he used to hit the culprit on the head. Unfazed by the head blow, the culprit broke away from the officer and ran onto a train, with the officer, bleeding from his wounds, in pursuit. Cornered in the crowded subway car, the youth turned and fled back onto the crowded platform, again pursued by the officer. On the platform, the youth turned once again and charged the officer with knife in hand. The officer fired twice, felling the culprit. All of this action took place during the peak of the evening rush hour. A few moments after the shooting, it was discovered that a young lady had been mortally wounded by one of the bullets fired by the officer. She was rushed to the hospital where she died on the operating table.

It was the most tragic type of shooting incident possible, the type of incident that the department and its members make every effort to avoid. You may be wondering, "Why did the officer get so involved over an incident involving $.50?" He got involved because it was his duty to get involved – the amount of the theft was not the issue. It would be totally unfair to the people who pay their fare every time they ride the train to permit others to ride for free and in so doing, violate the oath he took to uphold the law. It's easy for an officer in plainclothes to ignore many situations such as this one. After all, since the officer is in civilian clothes, very few people "make him." But these officers are selected on the basis of their past performance and the simple fact that they have proven to be trustworthy and do not require close supervision. Other factors are considered, of course, but the officer must be trustworthy. Without that particular trait, an officer is useless in plainclothes. Such officers could easily avoid taking police action in situations they know can easily become dangerous and stressful.

Consider two plainclothes officers on duty on a hot summer's night in a subway located in a poor neighborhood. They are on such duty in response to a large number of complaints received from fare payers claiming that there are many people jumping over turnstiles or going through exit gates to avoid paying their fare. The people from this poor neighborhood have been paying their fares religiously and it really makes them angry to see others not pay. So now here we have the two police officers dressed in plainclothes and on the scene to try to stem the tide of the free riders. They are only on the station five minutes when they observe four persons jump over the turnstiles just as the train is entering the station – perfect timing on the part of the jumpers. The two cops grab the four jumpers, showing their shields and announcing "You are under arrest" all at the same time. Within minutes, you have over one hundred people running into the station, surrounding the officers and trying to free the four jumpers. The poor cops hope their radios work as they call a "10-13" – an officer's call for assistance. Despite the excellent response of police units in "10-13" situations, a lot of heavy things can happen in a few minutes under such conditions. These anti-crime officers have real guts and we can't commend them enough for their valor and the job they do every day. Minor type crimes such as these "fare beats" do not constitute the bulk of transit police work. Quite the opposite is true – transit cops encounter the complete gamut of crime – from homicide, rape, robbery, sodomy, kidnapping, desertion from the armed forces, and right down to disorderly conduct. You name the crime, we have it. I want to make it crystal clear – most subway crime is serious and violent.

Regarding the tragic incident that resulted in the shooting death of an innocent young lady, true enough that it started out as a $.50 theft, but the thief's subsequent actions escalated into an attempted murder of a police officer who had to fire his weapon in order to save his own life. In fact, the culprit should have been charged with homicide for causing the young lady's death.

Another tragic shooting incident occurred while I was serving as the lieutenant-in-charge of the Firearms Training Unit. It concerned a rookie police officer that I'll call "Officer J.S." I first met this officer while I was working out of one of our ranges at the old Brooklyn Navy Yard. At that time, Officer J.S. was still on active duty as a quartermaster in the Navy and was stationed there. Since I had also been a Navy quartermaster and since we were both New Yorkers, we had things in common and became friends. A new examination was scheduled in the near future and I talked Officer J.S. into taking the entrance examination. He passed easily and in a short period of time, he left the Navy and was appointed to the Transit Police Department. I then saw him on several occasions when he visited the range as a recruit for pistol training. He also visited the range on his own time in an effort to further improve his shooting ability. I asked him if he was sorry he left the Navy to enter police work and he said, "No, Lou, you gave me good advice as one old quartermaster to another. As you said, the salary is good and the benefits are great. You also told me it was a ringside seat to the greatest show on earth. And it is – I love it!" It made me feel good to know that Officer J.S. was happy in the job.

After he graduated from the Police Academy, he was assigned to patrol duty in both Manhattan and the Bronx.

One day, while returning to his home in civilian clothes after a court appearance, he observed a male acting suspiciously in the Hunts Point IRT subway station in the Bronx. Officer J.S. identified himself as a police officer and was questioning the suspect about his actions when the suspect suddenly pulled a gun and shot the officer. Officer J.S. was struck in the shoulder and upper arm. The culprit fled upstairs into the busy street. The officer, bleeding heavily from his wounds and with his gun drawn, ran up the subway stairs in pursuit of the gunman. A city police officer was at the top of the subway stairs at the time and heard the sound of gunfire coming from the subway. He saw the culprit running from the subway and heard him shout to the city officer, "There's a madman down there with a gun shooting at everybody." Just then, the city cop saw Officer J.S. running up the stairs, bleeding, with a gun in his hand. The city cop fired, hitting Officer J.S. who fell, mortally wounded. Officer J.S. managed to gasp, "I'm on the job," before passing out. The poor city cop called a "10-13" on his portable radio and within moments, many police units were on the scene. The suspect was apprehended almost immediately and taken into custody for questioning. Officer J.S. was sped to the hospital in a city police radio car where he was rushed into surgery. Hundreds of police officers from the three city police forces – city, housing, and transit – responded to give blood, help in the investigation, and maintain a vigil for the wounded officer. The mayor, police commissioner, many high ranking officials, Transit Authority commissioners, as well as many concerned citizens, went to the hospital to offer their blood and their prayers. God called Officer J.S. home, ending his police career after only one year of service. He left a young wife and children and a big void in the Transit Police Department. Rest in peace, my friend.

Incidentally, the creep that caused his tragic death was wanted for several violent robbery crimes in the South Bronx and should have been charged with murder – it was his actions that caused the officer's death. But he wasn't!

Chapter 12

On a pleasant note regarding my assignment in the Firearms Unit, I determined that the department needed additional ranges to facilitate our training operations. I was fortunate enough to get three additional ranges, giving us a range in nearly every borough plus a large outdoor range in Newburg, NY. Having these ranges so located made it much easier for the members to report for firearms training and it helped save money for the city. The range in Newburg, NY was especially popular because many of the members resided in Rockland, Orange, and Sullivan counties. These members didn't have to travel all the way to the city on their off-duty time to qualify for firearms training. I obtained permission from my boss, Captain "Charlie D," commanding officer of the Police Academy, to purchase special work uniforms for our range officers. We even designed a special firearms patch to wear with these uniforms. We used Army, Navy, and Marine Corps tans with blue baseball caps that had crossed pistols as our insignia. We looked really sharp and it was good for morale – not only for us, but also for the members we trained. It gave us a professional touch!

I got a lot of help from Lieutenant "Frank Mc," the commanding officer in charge of the New York City Police Department Firearms Unit. Lieutenant "Frank Mc" is probably the foremost expert in firearms throughout the entire country. The city police outdoor range at Rodman's Neck in the Bronx is one of the finest firearms complexes in the world. Lieutenant Frank Mc never stops building and working, and since I haven't been to his range since I made captain over seven years ago, I don't know what other new twists he has added since then. But knowing him and his band of working troops, I'm sure it's seven times bigger and better than I remember it. "The Lou" and his men taught us a lot and we in turn taught our members in the same professional way. He also provided us with the use of a twelve-point firing range and the use of one of his buildings for administrative purposes. It was great duty for us while we were at Rodman's Neck, and it provided us with the opportunity for instituting both the combat and shotgun training courses – both of which benefited our members later in active patrol situations.

We also conducted tests of material that were later installed in the bulletproof token booths in the subways. The installation of these bulletproof booths greatly reduced the number of successful booth holdups and helped reduce the number of deaths and injuries to Transit Authority employees. Many tests were required in order to determine what caliber of bullets these booths could withstand. We had reached the point of making a final recommendation when we were notified by one of the chiefs to be prepared to stage a demonstration for the news media the next day! The site selected for the demonstration was the oldest pistol range in the city. It was located in the arsenal in Central Park and had been built around the time of the Civil War. The range lacked the electrical outlets that the army of press and television people needed for their equipment. The press put through a call and in no time, a truck arrived full of electricians and they installed all the needed outlets. We wouldn't have to worry about where to plug in the coffee pot anymore! I was amazed at the well known TV personalities that showed up to witness and record our ballistics tests. Doug Johnson and Chris Borgen were there, among others, and both gave us great coverage on the event.

Here's how we conducted the tests. We had samples of the bulletproof materials mounted in a steel frame placed down range. These steel frames were not perfect fits, so you had some impact weakness result from some of the higher caliber hits. Officer "Tony B," one of my range officers who was a crack shot, National Pistol Shooting Champ, and an ex-Marine sergeant, did most of the firing. After each shot, I would walk down range, examine the sample, and announce, "No penetration," circling the spot with a magic marker. I would also announce the caliber of the bullet – .22 caliber, .25 caliber, .32 caliber, .38 caliber, and .45 caliber. One un-expected sideshow almost developed that has remained a secret until now. When we got to the .45 caliber shot, Tony and I got a little carried away and decided to fire a .45 caliber submachine gun for special effect. This wasn't in the script, but we did it anyway. It was most dramatic and got everyone's attention -- especially mine! After Tony had fired a burst from the Thompson submachine gun, I walked slowly down range, afraid to look at the sample. Remember, the steel frame was not a perfect fit and the "rat-tat-tat" of impacting .45 caliber machine gun slugs could have shattered the sample as well as my assignment as a range lieutenant! Luckily, none of the slugs actually penetrated the sample, but the back part of the lexicon material was somewhat fragmented. In full view of the media and while the TV cameras were recording, I rubbed my hand across the back of the fragmented sample and winced as I felt a sharp sting. I felt some blood on my hand which I quickly concealed behind my back while I announced, "No penetration." There really wasn't, but it would not have looked good on TV to have the range officer dripping blood on the floor while proclaiming the material to be bulletproof! Chris Borgen, a former detective in the New York City Police Department, decided to ask me a few questions about the fragmentations on the back of the last sample. "Lieutenant, you say there is no penetration. What about the fragmentation on the back?" "Chris," I replied, "these are radial fractures caused by repeating, impacting slugs on a sample that is mounted in an imperfect frame. This could not happen to the finished product when it is mounted in a perfect setting."

Chris asked me if I would feel safe standing behind such a bulletproof device. I told him that particularly in these violent times, I would be delighted to have such a protective device on patrol. That concluded the interview and the demonstration – plus our little sideshow. All the television channels gave us tremendous coverage on the story and today, most of the booths, and the Transit Authority employees, have bulletproof protection.

I am proud to have been a member of the Firearms Unit and grateful that I had the honor of serving as its commanding officer. I hope I made some meaningful contributions to that splendid unit and want to express my thanks to all its members: you made it a pleasure to come to work each day.

Chapter 13

I was still serving in the Firearms Unit when the examination for police captain was given. The steady hours I was working made it easier to attend study classes. But the course itself was tough and the competition for the position was far stiffer than I had ever faced before. There were thirty young lieutenants in the department at the time. Almost all of them were under thirty years old and had risen through the ranks very rapidly. These guys were very, very sharp. Our instructor, Captain Mulhearn, referred to them as "The Whiz Kids," and they were! I seriously doubted that I would make the captain's list, but I was committed to try. This examination was the whole ball game. I had to make it if only to prove to Eileen and myself that making sergeant would eventually be worth it. The only way to win that argument was to earn a set of captain's bars.

The examination was held on a Saturday at Franklin K. Lane High School in Queens. It was an exceptionally hot day, so the classroom windows were all open to let in some air. It also let in lots of distracting noise since a ball game was in progress on the field directly below the classroom. The examination consisted of 135 multiple choice questions, many of which were quite verbose. Additionally, there were an unusually high number of math questions, something like eighteen of them. The four-hour time allotted for the test seemed hardly enough! The competition, the pressure, and the noise from the ball field all combined to make the test a memorable experience. With so many careers on the line, the final bell rang announcing the end of the grueling struggle. We were allowed to keep our copies of the test and a copy of our answer sheet – a form of Chinese torture since we would now have ample time, in the cold light of review, to see how many questions we really blew! As I said earlier, these tests are like a giant lottery -- you take your best shot and then hope for the best. So many really capable people just never "grab the brass ring" when it comes to test-taking, and they don't make the list. But that doesn't necessarily mean they are not qualified. Nevertheless, civil service examinations are a fair way of making selections for promotion. Not perfect, but fair and honest. It's just unfortunate that so many qualified people never get promoted.

It didn't take more than a few days for a set of unofficial answers to the exam to circulate. Some of the brainier members of the three police departments – city, transit, and housing – had gotten together and agreed on a set of tentative answers. Members of all three forces had taken the identical exam for captain. I guess we were finally accepted as equals! I took a copy of these answers home one night and after dinner, retreated to the basement to check my answers. Armed with a cup of coffee, having said a few fervent "Hail Mary's," and while seated beneath my photo of the *USS Bailey*, I marked my paper. I didn't feel too confident when I had finished, although I felt I had passed. I just couldn't tell if my grade was good enough to be promoted. I, as well as many others, would just have to wait several months to find out.

In the meantime, I spent many anxious days trying to figure out just who would be on the list. I hung on to the slimmest hopes imaginable. For example, a friend of mine who did very well on the test and had no doubts about making it, called me up to tell me this story. "John, I had a dream last night. In this dream, you and I both made it." I knew he wasn't a prophet, but I believed him and his story buoyed my hopes for months. The captain's list was finally published, two days before Christmas -- a great Christmas if you made it and a real bummer if you didn't! I was one of the fortunate ones, along with my friend the soothsayer. Go figure!

There were twenty-six vacancies in the rank of captain in our department at the time, so twenty-six of us were promoted to captain on January 23, 1972. As is the usual custom in police service, formal ceremonies were conducted and family members were invited to attend. A few of us "old timers" really stood out among all the young "Whiz Kids" getting their sets of captain's bars. But they earned them and as it turned out, became fine leaders. Two of them presently hold the rank of full inspector and three of them are deputy inspectors. My wife, Eileen, my son, Brian and his fiancée, Kathy, my daughter, Susan and our first grandchild, Aimee (age three months) were present to see me get those coveted bars. After the promotion ceremony was completed, we all went to dinner and over a lingering glass of wine, I remarked to Eileen, "I guess you understand now why I took the sergeant's promotion six years ago. I told you then I'd have you on Broadway, kid. And don't forget, a captain makes $6,000 more a year than lieutenants do. Who knows, maybe I'll make chief!" THAT SURE WAS A GREAT DAY!

I was again assigned to the patrol division which meant, once again, working around the clock and weekends. I wasn't given a command but was assigned instead as a duty relief captain covering Brooklyn and Queens. I filled in as a temporary district commander when the other captains were off or when they were on vacation. A real switch hitter! I knew all the years I had spent fighting for the troops would not endear me to the "big brass." They never expected me to make captain and to tread on their sacred ground as part of top management. To this day, the brass has never really accepted the fact – I will always be one of the troops in their eyes. You want to know something? Without the troops, there would be no brass and the job would never get done. So, I'm in good company by being held in high esteem by the troops.

Shortly after my promotion to captain, two of my best

friends, Detective Steve O'Connor and his lovely wife, Marie, gave a surprise party for me at their home in Neponsit, Queens. The party was well-attended by many friends and family members. They even had lyrics printed to the tune of "Hello, Dolly," hailing my promotion and proclaiming something like, "He's got the chief shaking, 'cause he's on his way to making ..." It was another great night!

News of the party, especially the jazz about me making chief, must have gotten back to the wrong people because shortly thereafter, I was transferred into the "Shoe-Fly Squad." What a shocker that was! Imagine me as an ex-PBA president, now a shoe-fly, faced with giving complaints to the men for patrol derelictions. I had no choice. It was either do it or quit – and I wasn't ready to retire then. I did that lousy, but necessary, job for about eighteen months. And I did the job well! It wasn't hard since all you had to do was think like a cop on patrol. I remembered what I did on certain posts when I was a cop – where I went for a smoke or a coffee break, etc. So I would go to those spots and many times, find some officers committing a minor patrol infraction. I'd wind up giving the cop a complaint and walk away muttering to myself, "You creep. You weren't perfect as a patrol cop. Why didn't you just forget it?" I couldn't, of course, since I was now a part of management and I had an obligation to exact proper patrol performance in that assignment. But it didn't make me feel any better!

I'm sure my personal stock with the troops took a nose dive, but it couldn't be helped. My one consolation while serving as a shoe-fly was that I never sank a cop for a heavy complaint. I only saw minor ones and although they hurt, too, there was no loss of job or serious penalty involved. Finally, the day came when I was called into the office of the deputy chief of patrol and given command of District 11 in the Bronx, next door to Yankee Stadium. The deputy chief of patrol made it quite clear that he had asked for me for that particular assignment because he believed I would make a good commanding officer. He quickly added, however, that many of the other bosses did not agree with him. The general feeling was that I was too much for the troops. The deputy chief warned me to be particularly alert and not get involved in any PBA politics, or I would lose my command in a hurry. He wished me luck, then took me inside to see his boss and reinstructed me in his presence. Can you imagine, even after eighteen months as a shoe-fly, they still didn't trust or accept me! The hell with them – I vowed to get the job done my way, with the cooperation of the troops. And it would be the best command in the department!

I reported to District 11 the next morning and was greeted with happy shouts of "Good morning, Captain – welcome aboard." After a guided tour of the district facilities by Police Officer Jerry "H," we entered the captain's office. Over a few cups of coffee, Jerry briefed me thoroughly on just about everything concerning the district. Before I knew it, the entire tour had passed. It was the beginning of a friendship and a professional working relationship that was to last for the three and a half years that I had the honor of serving as the commanding officer of the "one-one." Let me tell you about Officer Jerry "H." At the time I got to know Jerry, he had about ten years on the job, almost all of it as a patrol officer. Like me, Jerry was a Navy man. In fact, he joined the naval reserves upon his discharge from active Navy duty during the Vietnam war, and held the rank of chief radioman. Some of us referred to Jerry as "Chief" because of his Navy background. I can't say for sure that it was because of our similar Navy backgrounds that we hit it off so well together, but it didn't hurt! Jerry was very helpful to me in my development as commanding officer of District 11. I had much to learn about being the commanding officer since I was so out of touch after serving eighteen months as a shoe-fly. The administrative duties of a commanding officer were quite complex. In addition to providing leadership, a captain had to be a chaplain, a disciplinarian, a buffer between the troops and higher authority, a humanizer of department policy, a good guy, and sometimes, a bad guy – just like fathers everywhere. I think I was able to fulfill all of these roles fairly well, with the possible exception of the "bad guy" role. Such a role was particularly tough for me. Not that I wouldn't zap someone who was really guilty of a serious infraction – I most certainly would, and did. But in those areas of minor violations, I always empathized with the men and used a positive approach to bring about the desired correction or change of attitude. It invariably worked for me as the men "broke their shoes" to improve their performance, thereby improving the command's performance.

However, this approach was to lead to trouble for me with my bosses -- later on. I will cover that subject in detail later on in the story. For now, let me speak on the subject of developing an effective field command.

At the time I was assigned to District 11, district captains had very little command authority. This lack of command authority was due primarily to the *centralized command concept* in effect throughout the department at the time. The entire job was controlled from headquarters, which meant that many of the functions of command were essentially removed from the district and unit commanders. Centralized command was ineffective and downright embarrassing! As a captain, you had no real control of necessary command tools, including preparation and assignment of roll calls, change of tours, excusals, and deployment of manpower. It left us captains with a feeling of *piloting a plane with the automatic pilot on*. Innovative techniques and initiative could not exist. It resulted in stifling job satisfaction, and seriously hampered the field forces, morale, and esprit de corps. All the captains did the best they could under the circumstances, but it wasn't good enough – and the public suffered because of it. I had submitted a few reports through proper channels advocating a decentralization of authority to a command level. All such reports were returned to me with endorsements such as, "Not feasible at the time."

Meanwhile, violent crimes continued to soar without district commanders having any real input in overall department operations. What a waste! At the time I was promoted to captain, I was also elected president of the Captains Endowment Association. Therefore, I became actively involved in all matters concerning the captains and once again, found myself in the position of fighting for the welfare of others – and in so doing, hurting my own welfare! Make no mistake about it, if you represent a group of employees and in so doing, have to take an opposite position to top management, YOU get hurt. Maybe not immediately, for that would be too obvious, but you will get hurt! Why? Because these top management people personalize things and conclude that the leader of whatever organization is the one that is fighting them. In their minds, it's the organization leader's views, not the membership's views. The bosses conclude that the leader stirred up the troops and therefore, is a troublemaker. Silence the leader, and you silence the membership. Make an example of the leader and you effectively discourage others from fighting improper practices. Despite having full knowledge of the above-mentioned problems inherent in being the leader of the Captains Endowment Association, I continued to fight for all the captains' rights and general welfare – but it definitely stymied my own career. The rank of captain is the last step on the civil service ladder, which you can reach solely on the basis of a competitive civil service examination. Any rank obtained after captain is merely a captain detailed to serve in a designated higher rank. For example, a captain is detailed to serve as a deputy inspector, inspector, deputy chief, assistant chief, deputy chief of department, or chief of department. All higher-ranking officers are appointed after they have attained captaincy. They are detailed to serve in the higher rank and, of course, are given more authority and higher pay. Throughout my entire police career, I was usually wearing two hats – cop and advocate. I was president of the PBA, president of the State Police Conference, president of the Lieutenants Association, President of the Superior Officers Council (representing detectives, sergeants, lieutenants, captains, deputy inspectors, inspectors, and deputy chiefs) and finally, president of the Captains Endowment Association. It's strange that those people I came in contact with, sometimes in an abrasive way because of the issues, and that held really high, non-police positions, never took things personally. It was always some high-ranking member of the police department (really a captain, so detailed) that "zapped" me. Strange, but true! But that is getting a little ahead of my story. Let's get back to my role as commanding officer of District 11, and my aide de camp, Officer Jerry "H."

Chapter 14

I had been in command of District 11 only a few short months when the first scandal involving the Transit Police Department broke. Certain high-ranking officers were the subject of various charges of misconduct, particularly the chief. The entire investigation of the "alleged misconduct" charges was under investigation by the state prosecutor's office, headed by Mr. Maurice Nadjari. These were indeed dark days with gloomy incidents taking place every day for several months. The situation received wide coverage in the media and eventually ended with the chief being dismissed after pleading guilty to non-criminal departmental charges. He received a <u>severe</u> penalty that included a reduction in rank from chief of the department to captain, plus the total loss of his pension – after serving over thirty years without a blemish! Fortunately, the ex-chief fought the matter through the courts and won. The courts ordered the chief's pension be restored, retroactively to the date of his dismissal, plus the restoration of his title of chief of department.

In addition to the chief, every officer except one, above

the rank of captain, either resigned voluntarily or was forced to resign. The following ranks "walked the plank":

- One deputy chief
- Two assistant chief inspectors
- Four deputy chief inspectors
- Eight inspectors
- Ten deputy inspectors

Other ranks also suffered in the purge. Several captains, lieutenants, sergeants, detectives, and police officers put their papers in – well in advance of their planned retirement dates – rather than serve under conditions that prevailed under the new regime. The casualty rate was awesome, and department morale crumbled. [2]

These conditions continued for about one year and resulted in many procedural and personnel changes in the department. All of these departmental personnel changes occurred immediately after the department had reduced felony crime by 64%, and had been nationally proclaimed by the Vice President of the United States. The new chief appointed to command the department was an "outsider," Sanford D. Garelik. "Sandy" was a former Chief Inspector

---

[2] Editor's Note: I am pretty sure that my dad did not agree with how this whole incident was handled. But as many of us have learned in our own careers, a typical reaction to these situations is to bring in a new leadership team, rather than to find that leadership from within the existing organization. It is easy to "Monday Morning Quarterback" a decision, but as it turned out, the Transit Authority would have done much better having chosen new Transit Police Department leadership from within its own department.

in the New York City Police Department, the highest ranking uniformed officer in that department. He was also the former President of the City Council, which is the second highest elective office in the City of New York, right beneath the mayor. When Sandy's appointment was first announced, we accepted it as being a good thing for the department. After all, with both police experience and political expertise, our new chief was expected to lead us to even greater professional heights than we had already achieved. No small feat, but considering the new chief's background, we expected it.

Then things happened that were not anticipated by the new chief. Before I get to some of them, let me tell you about the first time I met the new chief. It was his first day on the job. I'll never forget it! It was March 17, 1975 – St. Patrick's Day in New York City. Everyone is just a little bit Irish on that day, in this town. We have a big parade up Fifth Avenue that starts at 44th Street and terminates at 86th Street and Lexington Avenue. I was working a 4 p.m.-to-midnight tour on that date, and was assigned to the parade crowd condition at 86th Street and Lexington Avenue, in civilian clothes. Since it was St. Patrick's Day, I was dressed pretty snappy, topping off my attire with a brand-new $125 white trench coat that Eileen had bought me for my birthday. I had planned to drop over on my meal period to a little bash being given by the Emerald Society after the parade ended. I never got there!

A major train derailment occurred on the West Side

Broadway #1 subway line involving several rush hour trains carrying several thousand passengers. Subway trains loaded with passengers were stuck in the dark, grimy, slippery subway underground, from 59th Street north to 96th Street. Upon receiving notification of the incident, I jumped into a radio motor patrol car driven by Officer John "F" from District 3 and sped to the scene of the incident. We arrived crosstown in about four minutes – quite a feat considering the parade and traffic conditions – even with a siren-screaming police vehicle! One quick look at conditions on the scene told me we had a "heavy" on our hands. I contacted the Operations Unit on John's portable radio and said as calmly as I could, "Charlie 11 [this meant the District 11 captain] to Operations. Total Transit presence on the scene at 86th Street at this time consists of me and my driver. Send multiple units forthwith with emergency lanterns and ladders. 10-4." Operations acknowledged my transmission and within minutes, the requested men and equipment were on the scene. I made the necessary assignments required to evacuate the passengers from the stalled trains. The ladders were needed to help the passengers get down from the trains to the track bed, where the men using the emergency lanterns and flashlights guided the passengers to safety – onto the station platforms and then upstairs to the street. In some instances, we were able to have trains pull abreast of the stalled trains and by using train seats as "gangways," remove the passengers to a running train that took them to a station where they could then exit to the streets. Block tickets were issued and alternative bus transportation provided. I kept Officer John "F" as my aide and radio communicator – he did a great job. He also made several useful suggestions that helped me, literally, "get the show on the road." But it was by no means a one-man show. The Fire Department, the City Police Department, and several departments of the Transit Authority all participated in the safe removal of several thousand people. It was a team effort all the way.

We had just gotten the situation at the 86th Street station under control, with all persons safely removed to the street area, when I was informed that our new chief was on the scene. I left the track area and reported to him. My brand-new $125 white trench coat was now covered with grime and steel dust, which I guess made a good impression on the chief – at least it showed I was working! He was being escorted by one of our inspectors, who introduced us. I briefed them on the situation, what action I had taken, and what I intended to do next. And I added, "Chief, under your direction, I'll proceed with units to 72nd Street to remove other passengers and cope with emerging conditions."

"Go right ahead, Captain, and keep me informed," replied the chief. We met up again later on at the 59th Street station, on the tracks, with the mayor and the fire commissioner. Both of them were in tuxedos, having responded to the scene from a formal dinner given by the Ancient Order of Hibernians. The fire commissioner approached me and asked my name and rank. I told him and he then said,

"Captain, I want you to walk the tracks from here to 86th Street and personally ascertain that there are no police, fire, or civilian people in the track area. When you have done so, notify us by radio and I'll give the order to restore the power." He added, "Have you got that?" I nodded affirmatively while looking from the fire commissioner to the mayor to our new chief. The chief added, "Go ahead, Captain." I took off up the dark road bed accompanied by Officer John "F," a Fire Department lieutenant, and a trainmaster. I realized it was an unusual order, but then again, so was the scene. Nevertheless, I decided after walking about 200 yards up the tracks to get additional confirmation. After all, the walk to 86th Street was bound to take an additional twenty-five minutes under the existing conditions. I didn't want the sole blame for holding up transit operations in the Big Apple for another twenty-five minutes if I had misinterpreted a verbal order. So, I got on the portable radio to Operations and said, "Charlie 11 to Operations. As I understand my orders from the fire commissioner, and concurred with by our new chief, I'm to proceed to 86th Street to ascertain if all areas are clear of personnel. After which, the power will be restored. I estimate my ETA at 86th Street to take another twenty-five minutes. Is there any change in those orders?" The Operations Unit 10-4'd me and added, "Wait one, Charlie 11." After a minute, Operations confirmed my orders, with no changes. That was fine with me and we then proceeded as directed. Halfway to 86th Street, I radioed again to ask if a similar unit had been sent southbound in order to expedite the order. The answer came back negative, so we did the surveillance by ourselves. At 86th Street, after ascertaining that the tracks were clear of all personnel, I gave the order to restore the power. After which all the choo-choo trains ran again, and the St. Paddy's Day celebrations continued!

That was how I first met the new chief. I couldn't have picked a better way to do it if I had planned it myself! And I made a hit with him right away. In fact, he called me at home to express his appreciation for a very professional job. Things were looking up, and continued to do so for several months. It just so happened during the new chief's early months on the job that just about every time a major incident took place requiring a captain on the scene, I was that captain. The chief usually responded also, so we met often under all kinds of incidents such as an officer being shot, a violent crime, floods, derailments, and major arrests. In these situations, no matter who else was on the scene, the chief would almost always confer with me about the incident.

Things started to change, however, when it became necessary for me, as president of the Captains Endowment Association, to oppose the chief on certain policies he was instituting. It started with opposing his order requiring all patrol captains to be in uniform and do supervisory patrol on foot. When that order was published, I asked for, and received, an immediate meeting with the chief. At the meeting, I informed the chief that we would not comply with his order for the following reasons:

1. If transit police captains patrolled in uniform, they would be unable to supervise effectively since they would be constantly stopped to answer questions and give directions to hundreds of passengers per tour.
2. In uniform, they would be subjected to making minor arrests, precluding the captains from performing their administrative and supervisory duties.
3. It wouldn't be feasible to pay captains their salaries, plus overtime, for their having to make minor arrests.

I mentioned that city police captains patrolled in uniform in radio cars, accompanied by a police officer as a driver. I then added that if the chief obtained patrol cars for us, we would comply with the order. The chief concluded the meeting with a promise that he would obtain the necessary cars. Within a few days, patrol cars were made available for patrol captains. The cars were "old bombs," obtained from other Transit Authority departments, and most of these cars did not have police radios. But they were cars, so we captains complied with the chief's order, and my stock started going downhill. Fortunes of war, I guess.

The next skirmish developed when the chief appointed an "executive assistant to the chief," a lawyer from Mr. Nadjari's office. The chief had the right to make such an appointment, and we had nothing personal against the gentleman appointed. We just felt that someone in the department should have been appointed as deputy chief instead. After the chief appointed his executive assistant, he decided to appoint a former high- ranking officer from the New York City Police Department as a "police consultant" to the chief. That appointment elevated our past skirmishes into a full- blown war. It amounted to another slap in the face, and the loss of two more high-ranking positions, to members of the Transit Police Department. The gap between the chief and the captains was thus widened, and the chief continued to isolate himself from his field commanders. The only persons who seemed to have his confidence were the two civilian members – his executive assistant and police consultant.

For awhile, the police consultant ran amok. He was definitely not the Cary Grant type, and he was everywhere, screaming and yelling at superior officers in front of the men. It seems he always found fault with whatever department function he was reviewing at the time. And as soon as this consultant reviewed the said function, some boss would be degraded, in front of his men. A lot of the bosses just could not put up with such tactics, and they retired. Which is exactly what the guy wanted – his form of attrition. Those of us survivors who decided to hang in there and refused to retire just because some outsiders wanted us to, continued to find the early sledding pretty rough. But we resolved that things were bound to improve, and they did.

Let me say something positive here about the police consultant. He was no jerk, had a law degree, knew police work, and was a sharp administrator. You had to do your homework before consulting him about anything connected with police work, but he sure didn't know, or care about, the decent way to treat subordinate police officers. He just didn't seem to like cops – I often wondered why he became one. Maybe he didn't like cops as a kid, or could be he saw too many of them eating apples off the fruit stand. Or maybe some cop kicked his tail for some minor thing when he was a kid. Or maybe some cop gave him a traffic ticket one time. I really don't know, but he sure didn't like cops, and cops sure didn't like him. It's too bad he had that flaw; he could have been one of the great ones. Anyway, we had to work with him for a while in order to get the job done, as he was the guy with the open door to the chief's office. If you wanted to work to save the department, you just had to go through the police consultant.

I got to know him pretty well as a result of certain circumstances. I had just returned from my vacation, a beautiful trip to Ireland, when the phone rang. It was the job and I was notified to be in the chief's office at 0900 the next morning. "You better be prepared to answer some tough questions about crime conditions in District 11," said the officer. Welcome home! I got up very early the next morning and went directly to District 11, arriving there around 0500 hours. I spent the next three hours "doing my homework" – reviewing crime reports, assignments made, and results obtained. I was ready to not only defend my position, but to go on the offensive. If you will permit a little immodesty -- we had done a good job in the "one-one." My aide, Officer Jerry "H" had helped me with statistics for the report and as I left for the hot seat, Jerry said, "Go get 'em, Skipper. I'll have the captain's gig alongside when you return."

"OK, Chief," I replied, "but have the crew ready to repel boarders in the interim. See you later."

And I left, taking the iron horse, the D train, to department headquarters in Brooklyn. I arrived about ten minutes before the meeting was scheduled to start, so I had a few minutes to visit with some of the headquarters people. "How's it going up in the "one-one," Cap? You're looking good. Hang in there." I managed to grab a quick cup of coffee and then went into the meeting room.

Chapter 15

I noticed immediately that the room was much too small for the number of people filing in. There was a huge desk in the center of the room with several chairs around it. I noticed two empty chairs opposite the center of the desk. I didn't know it at the time, but the two chairs were reserved for the police consultant and me. All the others at the meeting were regulars at such meetings and had to attend them every day. They all looked shell-shocked! We people in the field referred to these daily meetings as "laugh-ins." Not that they were "ha ha funny," but "strange funny." It seemed that every day, someone sat in that hot seat and got roasted. By now, the regulars were used to such things and were prepared for it, given the stacks of reports they all carried. The police consultant entered the room and the meeting started. First, he called for the report on overtime, comparing the figure with that reported the previous year. The captain controlling overtime rattled off his statistics like a West Point cadet, ending his report with, "I'm happy to report, sir, that we reduced the overtime factor by 15.4%."

"That's not nearly enough," growled the police consultant, "keep working on it."

Next came a report from a lieutenant in the detective division. The commanding officer of that division had just resigned, so the poor lieutenant was stuck giving the report. He didn't do too well and was ordered out of the room with a sharp reprimand from the police consultant, "Don't come back until you know your job." Some deputy inspector was up next with a report concerning a reorganization of the Operations Unit. He didn't do too well either, and at the end of his report, he was instructed to "find out why some cop's radio didn't work last night on Flatbush Avenue." I know it's important that the cops' radios work, for their lives might depend on them, but it wasn't the deputy inspector's fault. The problem was caused by the radios being incapable in some areas of sending and receiving transmissions due to subway conditions. The wires strung throughout the transit system to relay the sound signals from one relay station to another just don't always function properly, and therefore we continue to have communication breakdowns on portable radios. The manufacturer of the radios, along with the Transit Authority engineers, are continuously working on the problem in an effort to perfect the communication capability. Anyway, the deputy inspector had to take the rap that morning for the whole bloody mess!

Finally, it was my turn at the meeting, only they didn't come directly at me. The police consultant started it by asking the commanding officer of the patrol division about a robbery complaint on one of the stations in my command. My boss started to answer, but I interrupted him by saying, "Wait a minute, Chief. That's my ball park. I'll answer that." I faced the police consultant and said, "In the first place, I want to tell you about the present ethnic composition of the Bronx."

The police consultant replied, "You can't tell me anything about the ethnic composition of the Bronx. I was the borough commander up there."

"I think it's important to listen to what I have to say about it, Chief, because it has a lot to do with the crime problem," I said. I always called the consultant "Chief" out of courtesy for his former rank, not to make points.

"Get on with it," said the consultant.

"Traditionally, my command area was inhabited by a large Jewish and Irish populace. That population composition stayed static for many, many years and then underwent a dramatic change about five years ago. The Jews and the Irish moved out of the area – that is to say, the younger ones moved out, leaving the older ones in the neighborhood. These older persons, who had lived in the Bronx for many years, always had jobs or owned some sort of business. The new residents of the area were mostly black or Hispanic, many of them being poor and without jobs. The Jewish and the Irish residents that remained in the area were mostly the elderly ones whose children had married and moved away. I'm not a sociologist, so I can't answer why, but this new mix of people has resulted in a tremendous increase in crime,

with most of the victims being elderly and the culprits being young." I continued, "The 44 Precinct [the city police
precinct covering the area] six years ago was the second qui-
etest precinct in the Bronx. It is now the busiest precinct in
the Bronx, and the second busiest precinct in the entire city.
I'm not knocking the city police, and I'm sure they made
every effort to cope with the problem. Unfortunately, crime
still continued to soar in the 44 precinct. Now, the same
culprits the '44' gets on the rooftops, in the hallways, and in
the streets, I get in the subways! And I haven't received any
of the vast resources that were poured into the '44' to stem
the tide. So, what do you want from me?"

When I finished my little speech, you could hear a pin
drop. The guys were looking at me like I had just scored
the winning touchdown. The police consultant broke the
silence with a very good question. He asked, "Despite the
prevailing conditions, what steps have you taken, Captain?"
I read my crime reports -- dates, times and locations, de-
scriptions of culprits, assignments made, results obtained,
use of anti-crime officers, pending requests for additional
manpower and equipment -- and ended my report by adding that I needed another car for patrol. I noted that such a
car was available since another department unit parked their
car right upstairs on 161st Street, with no one allowed to
use it from 6:00 p.m. to 6:00 a.m. It just occupied space for
those twelve hours.

I said, "I would like to use that vehicle during those
hours it is sitting idle. I'd put two uniformed officers in it

and have them patrol certain high crime stations, getting out of the car and inspecting the stations. The vehicle would increase their mobility and number of stations they could patrol. By varying their patrol patterns, an appearance of police omnipresence would be created."

At this, the police consultant stood up and directed the patrol chief to make that car available to my command immediately. He shook my hand and congratulated me on an articulate and interesting report, adding that he wanted to talk to me again in the immediate future. He then concluded the meeting. Outside of his office, several of the guys waited to shake my hand and express their admiration for the way I "stood up." I didn't think that it went that well, but I accepted their praise, said good-bye, and went back to my command. I felt like a Happy Warrior, and very lucky!

About one week after that meeting with the police consultant, I received a call from one of his assistants. "Mr. 'C' would like to discuss something with you this afternoon. Be downtown around 3:00 p.m., in uniform." I was outside his office promptly at 3:00 p.m.; I didn't get to talk to him until 6:00 p.m. I notice while waiting that the guy was extremely busy. He kept going in and out of various offices, including the chief's, always with a stack of papers in his hands. He was like the guy in the juggling act with nine balls in the air, all at the same time, but never dropping any of them. At 6:00 p.m., he came over to where I was waiting and apologized for keeping me so long.

"Cap," he said, "I owe you a dinner. Let's go to Gage and Tolliver's."

"Chief," I said, "I'm not hungry and besides, their prices are outrageous."

He said, "Yes, but their food is great."

"I know, I've eaten there before. I'm just not hungry."

"OK," he said, "let's walk over to Court Street to another place I know. I'm starved."

I said, "I'll have coffee while you eat and we talk, Chief." Off we went, with me in uniform, on a five-block walk to the restaurant. Just about every ten feet, someone would stop me to ask some sort of a question, or to ask for directions. Despite such interruptions, we two didn't miss a beat. I mean we were talking police administration all the way. "What are your views on decentralization?" "How would you propose to administer a decentralized command?" "How would you prepare your roll calls?" "Would you need an increase in your present command quota?" "What about anti-crime?" "What about the use of detectives?" "Can you handle stakeouts?" "Do you have good clerical people?" "What are your heaviest crime periods?" "Where are your worst crime stations?" "Do you maintain contact with the city police captains in your area?" "How are the crowd conditions at Yankee Stadium?" And so it went. We talked all through the police consultants' dinner, well over two hours, despite the fact that we were constantly disturbed by many of the diners who knew him. This included the maître d', some assistant district attorneys, cops, and several members of the Board of Education. The guy knew a lot of people!

We finally got out of the restaurant and walked back to headquarters, talking all the way. "It was good meeting you, Captain, and I'm satisfied that you can handle a decentralized command. I'm not the chief, Sandy is. But I'll talk to him and get back to you in a few days."

I replied, "Just a few other things before you go, Chief. If Sandy gives me the job, I want a free hand in setting up and running the show. I also want the authority to establish flexible hours for my troops, and for myself. I want complete charge of excusals, tour changes, and squad realignments. That's about it."

"OK, John, I'll see what I can do and I'll get back to you in a few days." We said good night, hopped into the radio car parked alongside headquarters with Officer Jerry "H" at the wheel, and we headed north to the Bronx.

I filled Jerry in on what happened, and then the both of us started planning how we would handle decentralization in the "one-one." The next days were busy indeed. I'd get to the district at about 0700 hours and rarely went off duty before 1830 hours. Officer Jerry and I worked continuously on setting up the mechanics for decentralization of the command. Jerry was a tremendous asset to me. He was an ace on administrative details and I just could not have gotten the job done without his help. If I had the authority to do so, I would have promoted Jerry to at least a lieutenant. All I could do was designate him my administrative assistant, with no raise in pay! But Jerry didn't mind – he liked working on the new concept and he knew how much I valued and appreciated his efforts. That's all he wanted. I also had help from many others in the command. But I'm getting a little ahead of my story. I'll cover our District record in detail later on.

Let me get back to the inception of our decentralization project, which started about a week after my meeting with the police consultant. I'll never forget the date – it was October 8, 1975. Mr. "C" called and said, "I cleared the project with the chief. You have been selected as the first 'model district commander' and you will have full authority to run your command entirely on your own. Of course, we'll hold you fully accountable for the results."

"That's fair enough, Chief," I replied. He wished me good luck and said he would keep in touch. And I knew he would! I immediately placed myself on a flexible duty chart which permitted me to work duty hours best suited to ongoing police conditions within the confines of District 11. Such flexibility was necessary to plan implementation of the chief's order to establish a "model district concept" in this command. This included roll call procedures, redeployment of manpower, detective assignments, anti-crime assignments, duty tours, realignment of squads, and post realignments. Five days later, I received my first two detectives and the "one-one" squad was in business. On that same day, we instituted the "one-one" anti-crime unit with a complement of one sergeant and eight police officers. They were given specific cases and locations to work, and I hoped we'd get immediate results. The anti-crime guys had been select-ed on the basis of their uniform performance, desire to work anti-crime, and ethnic backgrounds. After all, I couldn't just have red-headed Irish guys, or Jewish guys, working in a predominantly black and Hispanic neighborhood and ex-pect them not to "get made." The first time these anti-crime guys reported for their new assignments was something else! They could easily have been mistaken for a band of renegades or hippies. But that's what we needed – guys who didn't look like cops. I wished them luck and sent them off to their assignments.

In ten days' time, that unit affected twenty-five arrests, seventeen of which were felonies. Every week thereafter, these anti-crime guys continued to "break their shoes" and brought in all kinds of good arrests. The "one-one" squad was also doing a great job. The squad made several rob-bery arrests, including the arrests of individuals responsible for approximately fifty token booth holdups throughout the transit system. Last, but certainly not least, the uniform force, the "troops in the trenches," did a fine job of not only reducing crime through diligent patrol, creating an appear-ance of police omnipresence, but they also came through with many outstanding arrests. All of us in the "one-one" functioned as a team with no superstars in order to obtain such excellent results. There was competition, sure, but no petty jealousy was evident, and morale soared. It was a good feeling.

I almost lost the chance to get the model district concept

off the ground, however, when I was changing a snow tire on my car, fell, and broke my right wrist. I was off duty at the time and as soon as it happened, I knew it was a bad break, in more ways than one. When I fell on it, the wrist bent back severely and shattered several bones. My wife drove me to the doctor's office for treatment and I kept on thinking on my way to the office that there goes my assignment as commanding officer of the "one-one." What good is a one-armed captain that can't write and can't drive? I thought I might have to retire. By the time we got to the doctor's office, I was convinced that my career as a police officer was ended. And all over changing a snow tire!

The doctor who treated me knew Eileen, since she worked as a medical receptionist in the building. So I received special attention. After studying the X-rays, he remarked, "Well, John, you did a good job on that wrist. It's going to be very difficult to reset. We'll do the best we can." He took hold of my arm, whereupon I turned my head and closed my eyes – no John Wayne was I! I had all I could do to keep from screaming. Damn, it hurt like hell when the doctor yanked that arm. He set it as best he could, casted it up to my shoulder, gave me some painkillers, and instructed me to rest as much as possible over the weekend. The doctor cautioned me to watch for any unusual swelling and then visit him the following Tuesday, if no unusual swelling occurred. Unfortunately, the wrist blew up on Sunday night, so I visited him on Monday before reporting for work. One look at my hand and the "Doc" cut through and removed the cast, replacing it with a new one. "It should be OK now and the swelling should start to level off. Take it easy for the next week or so." I didn't want to risk losing my command and decided to go to work. Wait a minute, I can't drive. How will I get there? I got it -- I'll call the district and have them assign one of the guys living near me as my driver.

I assigned Officer Herb "R" to the task and he picked me up in his car that morning. The poor guy had to listen to my account of the accident all the way to the Bronx. But at least he would have steady hours and weekends off for awhile driving the "old man." There was a staff meeting downtown that afternoon and I showed up with my arm in a sling. The police consultant and the chief were really impressed that I hadn't gone on the sick list. "Great example you are setting for the troops, John. We'll assign you a department car and a driver."

I replied, "I've already selected my driver but I'll take the offer on the department car."

"You've got it -- we appreciate your staying on the job." So it came to pass that I had a driver and a car for the three months that it took for the wrist to heal. It never healed completely, and I have very little strength in it, but at least I can turn it enough to get my change at the supermarket!

It was a very nice gesture on the part of the chief and the police consultant, assigning a department vehicle and letting me select my driver. It motivated me to do a better job as the commanding officer of the "one-one". Working really helped me to recover quicker than staying home. Every day,

I would take a little time out and sit in the porter's room, soaking my hand in Epsom salts, opening the hand a bit more each time. All the time I was in the porter's room, Officer Jerry would be with me taking dictation from me for my reports, patrol deployments, and ongoing plans. He was truly my right arm! Such was the spirit that prevailed in the "one-one."

Things were really going great, everyone's morale in the command soared, and we were getting positive results. Most of us were getting excellent job satisfaction out of our team efforts. Then, things took a bad turn for me, personally.

Chapter 16

As president of the Captains Endowment Association, I instituted two court actions against the chief, his police consultant, and the Transit Police Department -- never a popular move. One case was directed against the police consultant, who continued to give our members direct orders. We won that court case – at least for the record! Now he goes to the chief and the chief has someone in the department give the consultant's orders! The other court case came about as a result of the deputy chief's position being filled by yet another former high-ranking officer of the New York City Police Department. That made three top spots that they grabbed. It was a weird turnaround when you think about it. Here are three of New York City's highest ranking officers who no doubt, always opposed the merger of both police forces, breaking their shoes to join the Transit Police Department -- sort of a reverse consolidation. Of course, they grabbed the three top spots and managed to continue to draw their police department pensions. Quite a salary increase! All of which made us look like a bunch of incompetent jerks, totally lacking the ability to discharge the duties of higher rank. We couldn't, and we didn't, stand still for it! As president of the Captains Endowment Association, I instituted a special proceeding in the Supreme Court of the State of New York on November 8, 1976 to enjoin the appointment of Anthony V. Bouza as deputy chief of the New York City Transit Police. The proceeding was commenced by service of an order to show cause. Contained below is the Captains Endowment Association's preliminary statement:

This is a special proceeding commenced pursuant to Article 73 of the CPLR in the nature of a Writ of Mandamus and seeking preliminary and permanent injunctive relief to enjoin the appointment of Anthony V. Bouza as a "deputy chief" in the New York City Police Department.

The Facts

The petitioner, John R. Martin, sues individually and in his representative capacity as president of the Captains Endowment Association of the New York City Transit Police Department. The respondents (Chief Garelik and the New York City Transit Authority) on November 9, 1976, appointed the respondent, Anthony V. Bouza, as deputy chief of the New York City Police Department. At the time of the commencement of this special proceeding, Anthony V. Bouza was never a member of the uniformed force of the New York City Transit Police Department. He is a retired member, presently on terminal leave from the New York City Police Department, where he held the rank of assistant chief. It is conceded at oral argument by the respondents and in petition that the rank of "deputy chief" New York City Transit Police Department, is within the competitive class of civil service. The respondent, Anthony V. Bouza, is not eligible within the competitive class of the New York City Transit Police Department. The petitioner and the members of the Captains Endowment Association of the New York City Transit Police Department are eligible to obtain the civil service competitive classified rank of "deputy chief." Petitioners claim that the respondent's appointment is illegal and violative of the Civil Service Law, the Public Authority Law, and the Retirement and Social Security Law.

The Conclusion

The appointment of Anthony V. Bouza is illegal, and a permanent injunction should issue enjoining him from performing the duties and functions of said position, and directing his termination.

The above cited material is a condensed version of a thirteen-page legal brief submitted by our attorneys -- Schofield, Dienst & Hartnett -- and argued by Richard A. Dienst. Naturally, the chief and the Transit Authority also submitted legal briefs containing their arguments against our lawsuit. Since I do not have a copy of their arguments, I cannot reproduce it. On December 10, 1976, Supreme Court Justice Arnold L. Fein ruled that civil service law allows the Transit Authority to appoint a deputy chief either from within the ranks or from outside. The judge did not rule on the second part of the suit which concerned a violation of the Retirement and Social Security Law. Instead of a ruling, the judge commented, in part, "The issue here is the respondent's right to appoint Bouza, not his right to receive his full retirement allowance. Whether his appointment will require a diminution of his retirement allowance is a matter to be considered by the Commission."

The *New York Daily News* carried this account of Judge Fein's decision.

OK BOUZA'S TRANSIT POST

The appointment of Anthony V. Bouza as deputy chief of the New York City Transit Police Department was upheld yesterday in Manhattan Supreme Court. Bouza retired as assistant chief of the City Police Department to take the transit post. Bouza's appointment had been challenged by the Transit Police Captains Endowment Association, whose president, John R. Martin, challenged the appointment on the ground that the deputy chief's position was in a competitive class and should have been filled from within the department's ranks. Supreme Court Justice Arnold L. Fein ruled that civil service law allows the transit authority to appoint a deputy chief either from within or from outside the ranks. Fein did not rule on a second part of Martin's suit, which questioned Bouza's right to receive a $23,500 a year police department pension while being paid $43,000 yearly as the Transit Police deputy chief.

By Daniel O'Grady

In addition to losing the court case, we also lost on another matter for which a hearing was held by the City Civil Service Commission. Said matter was a proposal submitted by the Transit Authority to classify chief of the Transit Police Department in the exempt class, Rule X, under heading New York City Transit Authority. This Civil Service Commission hearing was conducted on March 2, 1977 and was attended by:

- Alphonse E. D'Ambrose, Chairman
- James W. Smith, Commissioner
- Josephine L. Cambino, Commissioner
- Nicholas La Porte, Jr., Secretary
- John G. deRoos, Senior Executive Officer, Transit Authority
- Leonard Wachsman, Civil Service Merit Council
- Robert P. Koch, Vice President, Captains Endowment Association, Transit Police Department
- Charles M. Mills, Secretary, Captains Endowment Association, Transit Police Department
- Alfred T. Vogel, Vice President, Civil Service Merit Council
- Sanford D. Garelik, Chief, Transit Police Department

I was on vacation and out of state at the time and therefore, unable to attend the hearing. There are twenty-six pages of minutes of that meeting, so I do not care to subject anyone to such a lengthy reading marathon of rather dull and dry material. I will refer, however, to some statements made at the hearing by Captain Bob Koch, vice president of the Captains Endowment Association, and Captain Charlie Mills, secretary of the Captains Endowment Association.

Captain Koch:

I am Robert P. Koch, vice president of the Captains Endowment Association. First of all, I'd like to point out that we do hold Chief Garelik's credentials in the highest regard. We have no objections to his past qualifications as chief inspector in the New York City Police Department. The position of chief of the Transit Police Department is not comparable to the position of commissioner of the New York City Police Department, which is under the administrative code as is required to come from the rank of captain, the competitive rank of captain. He can also be removed without a hearing and I do submit that it is comparable to that position; not to the position of commissioner. The Captains Endowment Association would have absolutely no objections to the appointment and classification of commissioner of Transit Police in the exempt class in that is a civilian position. We would have to object to the position of chief of the Transit Police as comparable to the position of commissioner of the New York City Police Department being classified as exempt as is the commissioner of the New York City Police Department. However, the position of chief of the Transit Police is the highest uniformed position, so, as such, it is not comparable.

Chairman D'Ambrose:

Is your objection than to the nomenclature or to the duties? Have you seen the duties of the incumbent?

Captain Koch:

I did not before today. I have requested that previously and we were told that the reasons and the duties would be given at the public hearing.

Chairman D'Ambrose:

Well, they have been available here and you could have gotten them from the secretary's office, but have you read them?

Captain Koch:

Yes, I did.

Chairman D'Ambrose:

Is it the duties statements that you have objections to or is it the title that you have objections to?

Captain Koch:

We object to the classification of the chief of the Transit Police Department being placed in the exempt class.

After Captain Koch spoke, here's what Captain Mills had to say:

Captain Mills:

I would just like to clear the air. The Captains Endowment Association, the Lieutenants Benevolent Association, and the Patrolman's Benevolent Association, are all opposed to the changing of the status. Now, we feel that the status should remain in the competitive class. I assume it is in the competitive status now.

Chairman D'Ambose:

Yes, it is.

Captain Mills:

And Mr. deRoos stated that Chief Garelik was appointed pending the changing of the classification to exempt status, so we take it to assume that the promotion was actually improper and against 1204 of the Public Authorities Law.

Chairman D'Ambrose:

No, there are provisions of law which allow for the creation of a position pending public hearings. Otherwise, government would come to a screeching halt.

Captain Mills:

We happen to go along with Mr. Vogel's feelings, that the chief of the Transit Police is a uniformed position, and to change it into an exempt status will kind of close a door. Patrolmen take a competitive examination and sergeants, lieutenants, and captains take them. To make it exempt for the chief's position, it's almost like saying a small boy can never be president of the USA. You're locking doors. That's our position. We feel that Chief Garelik is qualified, the duties as outlined are proper and we feel that possibly, Mr. deRoos should have been asking for a commissioner of Transit Police which would be a civilian and keep it in the exempt class and still maintain the rank of chief of the Transit Police Department as a uniformed rank.

Chairman D'Ambrose:

Again, let me ask you one question, if I may. If you change the title to some other title, would you change any of the duties?

Captain Mills:

We wouldn't change the title. We suggest an additional position. The title would remain the same. In other words, we don't want to lose the position of chief, Transit Police Department, but we feel that Chief Garelik, as stated, is comparable to the city police commissioner, and he should bear the title of commissioner but the title, chief, Transit Police Department, should remain a uniformed position, not closing the door for all entering the department. That is our position.

Despite the fine efforts by both Captain Koch and Captain Mills, coupled with stated objections from representatives of the Civil Service Merit Council, the Civil Service Commission placed the position of chief, Transit Police Department, in the exempt class. And we lost yet another battle; not the war, but another important battle!

As a direct result of my role as president of the Captains Endowment Association in instituting the aforementioned legal proceedings in a court of law, departmental charges were preferred against me. To the best of my recollection, here's what happened. I was scheduled to work a 1200 to 2000 tour of duty on the date I instituted the court action regarding the appointment of Deputy Chief Bouza. The manner in which the appointment was announced created even more tension between the chief and his subordinates. It happened via a press release on a Saturday afternoon, relayed through a court reporter to one of our court sergeants, who in turn notified one of our duty captains. The duty captain immediately notified me at home and gave me the bad news. The bad news of Bouza's appointment, which was to become effective the following Tuesday, also contained some good news. The good news was that eight captains would be designated deputy inspectors and three captains would be designated full inspectors. So, some good results had been obtained as a result of the Captains Endowment Association's efforts to convince the chief that these promotions were necessary. We couldn't fault the good news, and although we didn't necessarily agree with all of his choices, we realized that those choices were his prerogative. I thanked the duty captain for calling – although the call ruined the rest of my weekend – and went about the business of entertaining our company. That is to say, I went through the physical motions of entertaining the guests. Inwardly, I was churning. My mind kept dwelling on the "Bouza Problem" and what to do about it.

And so it went the rest of the weekend. I received several calls, not only from members of the CEA, but also from members of the other line organizations as well. All of the calls were in the same vein. "I heard about Bouza's appointment. Another city PD guy is grabbing another top spot. What are you going to do about it?" And so it went, all day Sunday, right up until bedtime. Naturally, my wife, Eileen, was upset, not just at the calls, but also because she realized that I had hoped to be promoted too. She knew that my role as president of the CEA had become the "kiss of death." I couldn't argue with her – she was dead right! I was up bright and early Monday morning, and after a shower and shave, I pondered our fate over a couple of cups of coffee and some toast. I couldn't come up with any clear path of action, so I decided to go in early in the hope that I would come up with one.

My mind was constantly on the problem during the drive into my command and when I arrived at the "one-one" about 0945 hours, I still had no concrete plan of action. Anyway, I was conferring with my anti-crime sergeant about crime conditions when the phone rang. The call was for me and it was from our CEA Vice President, Captain Bob Koch, who this time was on vacation. The phone conversation went something like this.

"John, it's Bob. Sorry I can't be with you today."

I replied, "It's OK, Bob. I know you are on vacation and have to leave town today. You handled the meeting at the Civil Service Commission while I was on vacation. I'll take care of this matter." After much discussion, it was agreed that I would go downtown to the PBA office to try to arrange an immediate meeting with the presidents of all the line organizations. I would seek to obtain their moral and financial support, consult with an attorney, and take whatever steps I deemed necessary in order to stop Bouza's appointment as deputy chief.

After I finished speaking with Bob, I called the PBA office and contacted the PBA president. He agreed to call an immediate meeting of all line organization presidents in his office later that morning. He also agreed to make the PBA law firm available and have an attorney present at the meeting. I thanked him for his support and informed him that I would be there within the hour. Before I left District 11, I informed the duty sergeant and the clerical officer on duty that I would be at the PBA office if anyone needed to contact me. I also contacted the Operations Unit and notified them that I would be at the PBA office and could be contacted there regarding police or other conditions. I left the "one-one" and went directly to the PBA office where I found all the other line organization officers plus the PBA attorney waiting. After some discussion and advice from the attorney, Dick Dienst, it was jointly agreed that we would institute an Article 78 Proceeding in Manhattan Supreme Court that very afternoon. Mr. Dienst said it would be necessary for me to go upstairs to his office to assist him prepare the necessary legal papers for court. I then thanked everyone for their support and went upstairs with the lawyer to his office.

The rest of the day was really heavy – giving legal depositions, Dick Dienst digging in and researching the necessary laws, secretaries madly typing reams of legal papers, Dick's two partners, Jack Schofield and Jim Bartnett, both former city cops, pitching in; news and TV reporters calling for statements, TV interviews being arranged, sending out for sandwiches, and so forth. It was really a busy, busy day! Despite all of the action in Dick's office, I still managed to contact the Operations Unit several times during the entire time I was there. I inquired about police conditions and gave them my exact location. Additionally, I spoke to a deputy inspector about changing a medical examination I was scheduled to take that afternoon. I gave the inspector the number of the PBA office so that he could contact me and confirm the cancellation – which he did. At about 1500 hours that afternoon, Doug Johnson of Channel 7 News came to the lawyer's office with his TV crew to interview us regarding the impending court action. It was shown on both the 6:00 p.m. and the 11:00 p.m. news that night. Several radio stations also broadcast the matter frequently throughout the entire day and evening, and all the news-papers carried the story for the next several days. In other words – it "hit the fan."

At approximately 1700 hours, after contacting the chief's office and extending them the courtesy of notification of our impending court action, Dick and I hustled across the few blocks to the Manhattan Supreme Court where a judge was waiting to hear our motion. We met the Transit Authority's top attorney there, Jim "Mc," a fine gentleman and a very capable lawyer. I think it was the first time he and I were on opposite sides. Our motion to have the appointment of Chief Bouza stayed that afternoon was denied by the judge. He agreed, however, to schedule a hearing for the next morning before the presiding judge. We returned to

Mr. Dienst's office around 6:00 p.m. and started working on additional legal papers for the next morning. After that work was finished, I returned to the PBA office to update the PBA president on the matter, when the phone rang – it was for me! My immediate boss (and a newly promoted full inspector) was calling to inquire why I was not at my command and why I had changed my duty tour without notifying him. He gave me a direct order to report forthwith to our internal affairs unit for an interview. I went to that "interview" accompanied by counsel, one Jack Schofield!

We arrived at the office of internal affairs at about 1915 hours and there we were met by the newly promoted inspector and the deputy inspector (also newly promoted) in charge of the internal affairs unit. I was asked if I would give an account of my activities for that day, which I did upon advice of counsel. Both inspectors asked me several questions pertaining to my duty tour – why I changed my tour hours, why I failed to notify my superior officer directly that I was performing CEA business, and additional questions of that nature. I replied, in substance, that I did not change my tour hours. I did get it in earlier than scheduled, but there is no rule against that. In fact, it should be commended. I noted that it was 2015 hours and I was still on duty, in their presence and at their orders. I was scheduled to go off duty at 2015 hours and I wanted it noted for the record.

The "interview" was concluded shortly thereafter and I went off duty, officially, at that time. We left their office, thanked Jack for representing me, said good night – adding that I would see him in the morning – and headed for home. What a day it had been! I was getting too old for that sort of stuff. I was back in court the next day with my counsel, Dick Dienst. Fortunately, it was my day off, so I was not concerned with being summoned by internal affairs. We didn't fare well in court at all, so Deputy Chief Bouza's appointment remained in effect. We also lost our appeal, so that was that. We accepted the judgment of the courts – that is the rule of the land. There was nothing personal in our battle. I did what I had to do as the elected leader of the Captains Endowment Association. I accepted the results although I wasn't thrilled with them. I was satisfied that I had done all that could have been done.

I didn't have time to dwell on the results of the court action as my duties as commanding officer of the "model district concept" in the "one-one" kept me fully occupied. Despite our differences, the chief left me in command and didn't put any undue pressure on me. Of course, our relationship was somewhat strained, and I did get a complaint and charges were filed against me for that first day in court. But I was assured that it had nothing to do with the court case – it was because I had not properly requested "release time" according to existing procedures. I was tried, and eventually convicted, on all three charges, which were:

1. Conduct prejudicial to the good order and efficiency of the department.
2. Changing duty tour without authority.
3. Failing to remain in my assigned location.

We appealed the conviction to the Transit Authority's chief hearing officer, the learned Judge Dan Gutman, who reversed the conviction, thereby clearing me of all preferred charges. The judge, in his ruling, referred to my "impeccable" record of over twenty-eight years' service without a single blemish and added that I was doing what I was elected to do – represent my membership. He suggested that the entire incident could have been handled without charges being preferred. Both Dick Dienst and Captain Bob Koch -- by then, the new president of the CEA -- represented me before Judge Gutman. You can see that they did their jobs well! I was very pleased with the results. I know that nobody is prefect, least of all me, and I know that somewhere along the way I've broken a few regulations I could have been "zapped" for, but I definitely didn't deserve one for this caper! I'm glad that Judge Gutman also saw it my way. The department accepted the judge's decision, and the matter was put to bed. I was left in command of the "one-one," where much was happening.

Chapter 17

I was working a day tour and I had to go to Brooklyn to attend a staff meeting. While at the meeting, we were informed that there was a hostage situation in progress aboard a southbound IRT train at the Chambers Street subway station. Several of us responded, including the chief of patrol. When we got to the scene, we were informed that a young Hispanic male was holding an elderly female hostage at knife point in the first car of the train. The youth had been observed committing a robbery aboard the train by two anti-crime officers who attempted to apprehend him. Before the officers could apprehend the culprit, he grabbed the woman, placed a knife to her throat, and forced the officers to withdraw. They radioed the condition to the communications unit, who in turn, ordered the trainmaster to hold the train at the Chambers Street station. All the passengers in the other cars of that train were safely removed, leaving the culprit, the hostage, and a female companion, several officers, some newspaper reporters, and some curious onlookers. Naturally, the entire station was sealed off and several specialized units responded to the condition --emergency service, hostage unit, chaplain's office, firearms unit, a SWAT team -- they were all present, waiting for the right moment to move in. The situation was extremely tense and filled with danger for the poor hostage and her companion. One false or imprudent move by anyone could trigger a violent reaction by the culprit.

Everyone was ordered to "cool it," while inside the first car, attempts were being made to negotiate the woman's release. One of the officers offered to exchange places with the hostage, but his offer was declined by the youth. Our chief was in that first car, talking his head off, trying to get the youth to free his victim in exchange for fair and humane treatment. Again, the youth refused. He demanded his lawyer, a woman, be present so that he could talk to her and decide what to do. He would not trust anyone else. Meanwhile, the IRT Line was at a standstill and thousands of passengers stranded while this creep made up his mind! Suddenly, the hostage became very irritated at the youth, who had been gently stroking her hair with one hand, while holding the sharp edge of the knife against her throat with the other hand. It was too much for the poor woman to bear, so she pushed his hand away from her head and demanded that he stop mussing her hair. It was a nervous moment for the culprit, who tensed up, pressed the knife to her throat, and screamed that he would kill her if she didn't shut up. We all froze momentarily, and then low-keyed it, talking calmly to the culprit. "Relax, kid, your lawyer has been located and will be here in a few minutes. Just don't hurt the lady." His lawyer had been located and was being rushed to the scene in a radio car. We prayed that she would arrive in time. She did! She talked to the youth for a few minutes, assuring him of fair treatment. He dropped his knife and released his victim, and about 100 cops plus 200 citizens and members of the press, sighed audibly. It was great to see a happy ending to a very dangerous situation!

The track record of the "one-one" for the first year of the "model district concept" was outstanding. The following excerpts from correspondence sent to Transit Police Headquarters helps to put their accomplishments in perspective.

Letter from Captain John R. Martin to Chief, NYC Transit Police Department, dated April 5, 1976

It is recommended that a general order, similar to the New York City Police Department's regarding unit citations, be instituted. (The NYPD order recognized that the lack of recognition for outstanding performance by entire units was a serious deficiency that tended to reduce morale, productivity, and esprit de corps.)

On or about November 23, 1975, District 11 was designated as a Model District with a full field control concept as per Chief Garelik's directive. Henceforth, all roll calls, all assignments and conditions within the command would be made by and with District 11 personnel. The department provided a redeployment of manpower allocation with complete authority to reassign members to squads and duty tours as needed. The total District 11 complement was a follows:

1 captain

4 lieutenants

12 sergeants

8 detectives

<u>154 patrolmen</u>

179 officers

The redeployment of a major percentage of police officers was the factor that immediately resulted in vastly improved police coverage. The concept was fully explained to all members of District 11 and full cooperation obtained. The troops executed exceptionally -- not only at the level of recorded performance but in other less noticeable areas such as planning, administration, and the desire to do an effective job.

A comparison of District 11 activity with the same time period last year (November 8, 1974 – March 31, 1975) indicated the following results, attributable to the implementation of the Model District concept:

- Felony complaints decreased from 325 to 196, a reduction of 40%
- Booth robberies decreased from 62 to 17, a reduction of 264%
- Total arrests increased from 207 to 523, an increase of 152%

- Total summonses issued increased from 1618 to 2845, an increase of 75%
- Total YDs issued increased from 229 to 539, an increase of 135%

It is my opinion that the above indicated statistics clearly merit a unit citation and awarding of a special breast bar to be worn by members of District 11. Over a year has passed since the inception of the model district program. This command was instrumental in the formulating of procedures and policies that have subsequently been implemented by the department for all model districts. Weekly, monthly, and on a continuous basis, reports concerning District 11 activities were forwarded to Department Headquarters for information and evaluation purposes. The overall results indicate much success in coping with emerging crime and other conditions within the confines of this command.

The crime statistics speak for themselves and are a clear and definite indication of the "can do" spirit of all personnel of this command. The uniform force in conjunction with anti-crime and district detectives, as well as other department units, all combined their efforts to improve police service and protection. The district stakeout unit, anti-crime unit, roll call unit, and crime analysis unit are but a few of the programs initiated to aid in combating crime successfully within this command. Various forms of directed patrol and concerted patrol procedures have been instituted to further

improve patrol performance. Additionally, manpower deployment and squad realignments were made to provide greater
increased visible uniform presence on all tours as well as
greater flexibility to meet new or ongoing crime conditions
within this command.

In any evaluation of the efforts of this or any command,
other variables besides pure statistics must be considered.
Increases in both federal and local crime statistics; heavy
crowd conditions at sport and other events conducted at
Yankee Stadium; the fact that a substantial number of former inhabitants of the east and south Bronx now reside in
areas encompassed by this command; the general socio-
economic makeup of the geographical area surrounding the
patrol area of this command (Fort Apache of the Bronx has
now moved into this command's area); the overtime record
of the command which reflects the high cooperation of all
members in curtailing overtime in accordance with department policy. These are but a few of the other important
variables that should be considered when evaluating a command's efficiency.

As indicated throughout this report, the success of District
11 resulted through **teamwork,** as demonstrated by all
members of the command. Some members, who prior to
the implementation of the model concept were considered
passive or non-productive, have over the past year been
motivated to increase their productivity and have become

active team members in this command. To single out a few members of this command for "outstanding work" would be demoralizing to the continuing outstanding efforts of all members.

I received a letter from Chief Garelik, dated August 11, 1976, in which he said, "The performance of the District 11 command has been commendable with respect to overall accomplishments. It is with regret that time and circumstance do not permit me to afford personal recognition to all members of my department who have performed admirably in the past."

In May of 1977, we began to see an increase in crime on buses running on lines parallel and adjacent to subway trains within District 11. I met with executive personnel of the Manhattan and Bronx Surface Transit Operating Authority (MaBSTOA) and we jointly came up with a plan that we believed would decrease crime on the bus lines without compromising the safety of our subways. The plan was predicated on obtaining a few cars or vans from MaBSTOA. A combination of uniformed officers and anti-crime unit officers were assigned to the vehicles in order to maintain a visible, as well as a covert, presence. All officers assigned to these vehicles were directed to inform bus dispatchers that they were covering the routes and could be contacted by radio or by a pre-established signal, such as flashing or blinking lights by the buses. The vehicles were in operation on a twenty-four hour basis, giving coverage to the bus routes and subway lines. Results were immediate. Unfortunately, the chief terminated the program a short time after we launched it, reassigning the vehicles from use by District 11 personnel to a city wide anti-crime unit.

There is no question in my mind that the bus patrols devised and instituted in the "one-one" at the time were most effective. These bus patrols were necessary in order to afford adequate police protection to the bus riding public, and the bus drivers. These bus passengers are entitled to such protection. After all, they pay the same fare as a subway rider. Why discriminate against the bus riders? They are in a sort of limbo and since buses run on the streets, the Transit Authority traditionally tried to refer all bus complaints to the city police. Most times, the city police would refer them back to the transit police since it was a "transit condition." Thus, the bus riding public was caught in the middle. Our plan provided police protection for both subway and bus riders by having patrols cover both modes of transportation, and the plan did not require additional manpower or equipment since we obtained free use of the MaBSTOA vehicles. But the big bosses didn't like my tactics, and so it was "farmed out" to another department unit. At least we were successful getting the department to accept its responsibility and make some bus assignments.

I should add that prior to making the aforementioned bus patrol assignments, two of my men had attended a community meeting at which community members demanded transit police protection on the bus lines. I subsequently met with the chairperson of that committee and promised to help – which I did! For some reason, however, the Transit Police Department desperately tries to avoid police responsibility for the bus lines. I can't understand such a strange paradox. After all, the department happily accepts police responsibility for the subways. Do they think we will drown in a sea of fresh air if transit police are assigned to bus conditions on the street?

Despite the good results obtained and the professional effort by some department members, the transit police bus coverage was drastically reduced. And shortly thereafter, I was transferred from the "one-one" house. The members of that command gave me a testimonial dinner – the first time a captain had ever gotten a testimonial dinner for being transferred. The dinner was held at the Marina Del Rey Restaurant in the Bronx. Of course, my wife Eileen, my daughter Susan, my son-in-law Bob, my son Brian, and my daughter-in-law Kathy, were all there to witness and enjoy such a tremendous tribute. The guys even had the Emerald Society Bag Piper Band for the occasion. It was truly a NIGHT TO REMEMBER!

The highlight of the evening took place when Officer Jerry "H," the "Chief," presented three plaques to me with the following inscriptions:

1
CAPTAIN JOHN R. MARTIN
COMMANDING OFFICER
OF THE 11TH TRANSIT POLICE DISTRICT

"The man who made the job. In recognition of your successful efforts of innovation and modernization of the Transit Police Department. A modern Pioneer."
Members of the 11th Transit Police District

2
CAPTAIN JOHN MARTIN

"In appreciation for that Guidance, Thoughtfulness and Consideration."
Shown to the Men of C.W.P.S. – District 11

3
CAPTAIN JOHN R. MARTIN

"In recognition of his interest and concern for his fellow police officers and his untiring efforts in their behalf."
Presented by the Emerald Society
New York City Transit Police Department
Matthew T. Walsh, President
July 15, 1977

I must admit, I felt proud to have been so well-regarded by the troops. I know that without regard by the troops, who after all, do the "gut job," the best results can never be obtained. I know further that the best way to lead is with a soft touch that includes empathy, compassion, and a genuine concern for your men. We all proved that concept in the "one-one." So after three and a half years as commanding officer of the "one-one," I was transferred just across the river to the "Big Three House" in Harlem. I hated to leave District 11, mainly because of the great guys I had the pleasure of working with. What a job they had done for me! And more importantly, what a great job they did for the riding public and the Transit Police Department. Mere words could never adequately describe how well they functioned, so I'll revert to an old Navy signal code to describe their effort: "TARE, VICTOR, GEORGE" – which means "WELL DONE."

Chapter 18

Ididn't exactly consider my transfer to District 3 as the highlight of my career. And I went there with some reservations about just how long I would survive as the commanding officer of "The Big Three House." District 3 had a reputation similar to "F Troop," mainly because some of its members (including me) were assigned to that command against their will. It didn't take me long however, to realize that such a reputation was undeserved. "The Big Three House" was a crack outfit! The troops were honed to a razor edge – meaning they were sharp. They had to be, because so were the bad guys. Most of my time during my first few weeks in District 3 was spent on administrative chores. I reviewed my personnel roster, squad alignments, radio car assignments, clerical assignments, roll call unit, school conditions, and anti-crime assignments. I also reviewed the current crime reports and manpower deployments. I interviewed my lieutenants, sergeants, and records officers in order to get a clear picture of crime conditions in the district before making any changes.

At the end of those two weeks, I was ready to make certain changes and establish my command policy. One of the very first things that I did was to put more men into the district's anti-crime unit. I did so because I am a firm believer in and advocate of anti-crime tactics. Anti-crime is one of the most effective weapons in police arsenals – provided, of course, the men work at it. We had no problem in "The Big Three House" with getting the men to work at anti-crime. These guys loved the assignment and the results they obtained were fantastic. I had about five times more volunteers for anti-crime than I could possibly use, so in order to give my uniformed men a taste, I would make daily plainclothes assignments in addition to anti-crime. We got very good results with these plainclothes assignments, and it was good training for the uniformed officers. I believe such assignments made them much more aware of the actions, locations, MOs, and identities of "The Bad Guys." Officers assigned to anti-crime/plainclothes units had the advantage of not being known or observed, most of the time, which resulted in the opportunity to make many arrests for crimes in progress. Naturally, the guys had to become actors – rehearsing, studying, and acting out their designated roles on patrol. They were hippies, bums, businessmen, students, telephone repairmen. You name it, these guys portrayed it!

It was really difficult to "make them," even for the bad guys. Certainly, there were times when they did "get made." It just can't be avoided sometimes, and don't forget, the enemy is always very streetwise. And it's even tougher not to "get made" in the subways. Here are some of the reasons why:

1. You don't have as much room to blend into the surroundings in many areas of the transit system.

2. During non-rush hours, you really stand out if you let a few trains go by and remain on a deserted platform.

3. If you send two white cops to an all black area, chances are they will "be made" in 0-eight flat. Same thing if you send one black and one white cop there. One black and one Hispanic cop might work.

4. Many crimes take place on moving trains, and getting officers close enough to observe these crimes and not get made is difficult.

5. It's very hard to develop informants in the subway since the population is transient and the grassroots element is removed from the crime scene.

6. A method of rapid escape is readily available. The culprits have many ways to go. Take a train north or south. Get lost in the crowds. Run up any number of street stairways, or at some stations, escape into a big department store.

There are additional reasons why it is difficult to observe, without being observed, on the transit system, but listing them all is kind of pointless. We are aware of them and it's our job to cope with them – and we do! The guys are always coming up with new ideas to improve effectiveness. Some of these ideas just can't be approved by the department, even though they could conceivably wipe out crime, because they would be "slightly illegal." You can't be "slightly illegal" any more than a woman can be "slightly pregnant." So, the department must ignore such proposals and stay within lawful guidelines to get the job done. I wish the bad guys would give their victims the same courtesy.

Having increased the size of my anti-crime and plain-clothes assignments, I next wanted to make sure that I had qualified sergeants to supervise these units. It turned out that I needn't have worried on that score, since the sergeant in charge of District 3 anti-crime was very qualified. I saw no reason to make a change there merely because I hadn't put him there. My predecessor had made an excellent choice of the anti-crime sergeant, so I stayed with it. I'm delighted that I did. I assigned an additional sergeant to anti-crime due to the increased size of that unit, coupled with the need to deploy more evening and night assignments. I determined to do something special for the uniformed force, not only to improve their effectiveness, but also to improve their morale and esprit de corps as well. As I said before, the uniformed force is the backbone of any police organization. They are the department's "Combat Infantrymen" -- "the troops in the trenches," for without them, the department's mission could never be accomplished. They deserved every consideration we could give them to make their job not only easier, but also to provide them with a sense of pride. I wanted them to know how important a role they played in the everyday operations of the department.

I wanted them to know that by doing their job diligently – being alert on patrol and courteous to people they encountered on patrol – they would be doing a helluva job. I reminded them that so many times on patrol, they prevent some violent crimes from happening just by being visible. I know it doesn't show up in the department records as a preventive crime, but that's what diligent patrol does. It prevents crime, and that's the name of the game. And although we know that total prevention of crime is impossible, we can and we must strive, with varied combinations of our police resources, to prevent as much crime as possible. We police officials cannot overstress the importance of crime prevention. That is why the uniformed force is so important to the total police effort. That is why we police officials must continuously boost the morale and effectiveness of the uniformed force – so that we may raise the level of protection to the public. A public that derives little satisfaction when police officers make arrests after they, the public, suffer an injury as a result of a crime committed against them. The public would prefer not to have had the crime, and the injury, occur in the first place. In other words, the public prefers CRIME PREVENTION!

This is the very reason why crime prevention must be stressed, refined, and innovated. Police stories, motion pictures, and television continue to glamorize police detectives, many times at the expense of the uniformed force. Such portrayals delude the public. One program that I believe "tells it like it is" is *Police Story*.[3] Their stories always point out the importance of the uniformed force, bringing detective, anti-crime and plainclothes into the action with proper perspective, in support of the main line – the uniformed force.

In emphasizing the importance of the uniformed force, I hope I have not offended the detectives, and anti-crime and plainclothes members. I have already cited the importance of their roles earlier in this chapter, and I was a detective for six years, so I know how important they are. They are the ones who have to move in after the crime has already happened and the trail grows colder with every passing minute. They are the ones that must reconstruct, interview, locate culprits, interrogate, narrow down the number of suspects, conduct lineups, get culprits identified, get victim/witnesses to prosecute, and finally, present the case in court. I gladly acknowledge the importance of detectives and anti-crime and plainclothes personnel, but the major deterrent in crime prevention remains the uniformed force.

When police commanders coordinate their efforts by utilizing a "team concept," the best possible results are achieved. I believe we obtained such concrete results using teamwork in both the "one-one" and the "Big Three

---

3 Editor's Note: *Police Story* is a television crime drama that aired on NBC from 1973 through 1978. The show was the creation of author and former policeman Joseph Wambaugh. It represented a major step forward in the realistic depiction of police work and violence on network TV.

House." I'm content to "stand on the record" of both of those commands. I told you in some detail of the results obtained in District 11. Now, I wish to detail some of the cases and results achieved in District 3. To be concise, I am mentioning only some of the cases and some of the officers. But I'm really paying tribute to the entire command because everyone contributed!

To do that, I am going to take excerpts from a report I submitted when I was informed of my impending transfer out of the "Big Three House," after having served approximately a year and a half as the commanding officer. The transfer was ordered primarily as a result of my continued practice of "going to bat" for my men. The brass disapproved of my leadership style, which they viewed as inconsistent with department and command area policy. In short, they thought I was too soft on discipline! I did not, and still don't, agree with them, so I submitted a detailed report to clearly document the outstanding record achieved by the officers of District 3.

Letter from Captain John R. Martin to Chief, NYC Transit Police Department, dated November 24, 1978

EVALUATION OF DISTRICT 3 OVERALL PERFORMANCE

On or about June 15, 1977, I was placed in command of District 3. At that time, the District 3 complement was as follows:

1 captain
6 lieutenants
10 sergeants
<u>160</u> police officers
177 total officers

Currently, the District 3 complement is:

1 captain
6 lieutenants
9 sergeants
<u>139</u> police officers
155 total officers

The complement assigned to District 3 in June of 1977 at 177 officers was sufficient in numerical strength to effectively fulfill the district's mission and the Transit Police Department's objectives of service and protection to the public and Transit Authority employees.

Comments on 1977 Results

Since most felony crime in this command occurs between the hours of 10:00 a.m. and 11 p.m., we have structured our manpower accordingly. Such deployment is generally constant throughout the school year, and when schools close, members of the Traffic Control Unit are reassigned. Our manpower deployment permitted daily plainclothes assignments from the roll call, on a rotating basis. These plainclothes assignments complemented the command's normal anti-crime assignments and provided field training for members normally assigned to uniformed patrol. Morale soared as did quality arrests, while there was a general decline in the number of open felony complaints.

District 3 members continued to maintain the effectiveness that earned them the Unit Citation in 1976. Although the numerical reduction in open felony complaints was small (five), we were competing with our own outstanding 1976 record. Additionally, felony arrests by the command's anti-crime unit were up by 117% and misdemeanor arrests were up by 90% – a further indication of increased productivity in 1977 and a clear and definite indication of the "can do" spirit of all personnel of this command. This unit's patrol force continued to perform diligently, and most effectively, the multiplicity of tasks assigned to them. In addition to many outstanding arrests, patrol force members coordinated their directed patrol assignments with members of the anti-crime and detective units, thereby improving those units' effectiveness. Valuable feedback was supplied to both the anti-crime and detective units by the uniformed members, resulting in additional arrests. Suffice to say, as police experts agree, "The patrol force is the backbone and combat infantry of the police department; all other police units are subordinate to them."

Effective September 1977, two two-man detective teams were assigned to this command. So far the results obtained have been positive and cover such areas as arrest, criminal identification, fingerprinting, case clearance, interviews and full cooperation with the patrol force and other department units. The outstanding results obtained by the members of District 3 were predicated on teamwork, and based on their outstanding performance, it is recommended that District 3 be awarded the Unit Citation for 1977.

Comments on 1978 Results

Since the District complement in June 1977 of 177 officers was adequate, no additional manpower was needed or requested. I determined, however, that certain changes were needed in manpower deployment in order to meet emerging crime conditions. The traffic control unit was reduced from nineteen to fourteen, while the anti-crime unit was increased from twelve to eighteen. These changes were necessary in order to cope with an increase in the number of robberies and grand larcenies that were occurring in the command, coupled with the loss of district detectives at the time. Felony arrests were increased by 47% and misdemeanor arrests were increased by 100% since increasing and redeploying the anti-crime unit to meet emerging crime conditions.

The performance by uniformed members also improved in 1978 with arrests, summonses, and YDs all continuing to increase, in spite of a 14% reduction in manpower. Open felony complaints increased over the 1976 level, due in large part to the reduction in manpower, and we have realigned our manpower in an effort to reverse that trend.

Concluding Comments

Each commanding officer will differ in priorities, type of assignments, number of officers in specialized assignments, etc. in order to accomplish a district's mission. And each commanding officer may differ in leadership style as well. General Lee was different from General Grant, and General Bradley different from General Patton. Certainly, President Truman was different from President Eisenhower. I favor the Lee, Bradley, and Eisenhower style of humanized leadership in discharging my command duties. I maintain it gets positive results and when the men are treated fairly, they do a better job in serving the public interest.

District 3 is a particularly sensitive command, and has been for many years, for a few reasons:
1. It is located in the heart of the ghetto.
2. Some members have been assigned to the command against their will.
3. It is a high crime area.

Although none of the reasons listed above is unique in police work, they are factors to be considered in order to motivate personnel effectively. When a unit executes effectively and gets positive results, the discipline factor is "built in" – ruling with an "iron fist" is not a requirement for success.

Leadership style should be judged on overall effectiveness, not philosophy, and that effectiveness should include taking the "troops' temperature" when it comes to morale and esprit de corps.

My aim since taking command of District 3 was getting improved performance, and as the record shows, we achieved that objective.

I am compelled to write something about a very fine gentleman and true friend whom I met while assigned to District 3. Everyone called him Jimmy and he was in charge of custodial duties in the district. He was also a deputy inspector in the auxiliary police, City of New York – a rank and duties that Jim did not take lightly. And he worked very hard at it. Every Sunday, his day off from his regular job, Jim would don his police inspector's uniform and patrol the streets of Harlem. He gave special attention to the street crossings in the vicinity of the many churches in his area, including his own. He also performed police duty during the "blackout" of 1977 and on many other occasions. So you can see that Jim understood police work. As a religious man, he also understood human relations, fair treatment, and the dignity of mankind. We had many conversations concerning the morale and fair treatment of the members of District 3 and Jimmy always found a way to let me know how conditions were in "the locker room." He would never mention specific individuals, just point out a general type of problem I might wish to look into. For example, he would say, "Hey, Cap, one of your steady post men on the late tour has made a lot of very good arrests. He's a little disappointed that he doesn't get any plainclothes assignments." I would then determine who the officer was, check his arrest activity (which was usually as good as Jimmy said it was), then give the officer some plainclothes assignments. The problem was solved and the officer's morale improved since he received recognition for his work. And at the same time, the district arrest record was improved. Jim would go to bat only for those guys that deserved it, and that was why I respected his judgment.

When Jimmy heard I was going to be transferred, he went to bat for me with some pretty powerful political, community, and church leaders, all of whom wanted me retained as the commanding officer of the "Big Three House." I visited the pastor of Saint Martin's Church seeking spiritual advice since the Reverend Doctor had been a New York City Police chaplain for over twenty years. His advice and counsel were exactly what I needed to restore faith in my ability and regain my self-confidence. Without the Reverend's guidance, I very probably would have retired when transferred. I'm grateful to the Reverend that I didn't.

I just want to add a few more stories about my duty in Harlem. First of all, let me make it crystal clear that I loved working there as the commanding officer. It gave me many opportunities to meet and work with so many fine people from all walks of life. I had many an occasion to meet with not only residents of Harlem, but also those from the communities of Washington Heights, Inwood, and Riverdale, since my area of responsibility encompassed all of these communities. Our patrol area extended north from 66th Street and Broadway to 242nd Street and Broadway in Riverdale. It was necessary for me on a regular basis to attend community and precinct council meetings. These meetings were always well attended by civic-minded people who wanted to work with the police agencies for the common good of all concerned. It was also an excellent opportunity to explain to them what we were doing about crime and other police-related problems. These meetings gave commanding officers an opportunity to explain things like assignment priorities, available manpower, police equipment, and legal procedures. The community members, in turn, could bring matters to our attention that we were unaware of, or not paying enough attention to. These meetings were a two-way street, beneficial to both parties. I enjoyed attending them, and I enjoyed the people I met at those meetings. In Harlem, as is true of other neighborhoods, the vast majority of the people are decent, hard-working, and civic-minded. I loved working there, as did most of my men. I wish I was still there as the CO of "The Big Three House." Now back to some cop stories.

Chapter 19

The night of the "blackout" in July of 1977, I had just arrived at home after doing a day tour and was about to have dinner when the TV news announced a massive power failure in the city. I said to Eileen, "Hurry up with dinner, hon; I'll have to put my uniform on and go back to work."

Just then, the phone rang. It was a sergeant from the communications unit.

"Cap, everyone is ordered back in."

I replied, "Ok, I'm on my way." I ate dinner, took a quick shower, and jumped into my uniform, after which I said goodbye to Eileen. By then, she was getting ready for a bridge game with Sally, Dot, and Joy, her regular bridge group. "Have fun, girls -- I don't think I'll be home before morning. Hon, don't wait up for me."

And off I went, back to the Big Apple. As I drove along, I pondered what had to be done and started making some preliminary plans to cope with the situation. We had a "blackout" once before, about twelve years ago when I was a detective. I didn't have the responsibility then of having to develop a plan and give other people orders, so the feeling was entirely different this time. By the time I got to District 3, I had some plans ready to implement and was starting to look forward to the impending challenge. It was just starting to get dark as I pulled my private car into 146th Street, just off the corner of St. Nicholas Avenue. I noticed that many more people were on that block than normal, so I took my uniform cap off and sort of sneaked out of the car. It seemed a prudent idea at the time not to let anyone know that the car belonged to a police captain! I liked the car and hoped to find it in working order if and when I got back to it.

Anyway, I got out of the car without too much notice and proceeded across the street to the subway entrance. The first unusual thing I noticed as I descended the stairs was that the lights were out and it was pitch black. I mean, you couldn't see your hand in front of you. So there I was, light-ing matches to see where I was going -- I left my flashlight in the car -- and all the while keeping my hand on my re-volver so I didn't get ripped off by someone lurking in the darkness. Luckily, no one was down there at the time. When I got to the bottom of the stairway, I found all the gates locked and I couldn't get into the subway. I noticed that the entire subway was in total darkness and realized that one of the first things we would have to do would include rigging some kind of emergency lights. I went back upstairs to the street and decided to walk to the entrance at 145th Street and St. Nick which I thought would certainly be open. I had only taken a few steps when I noticed hundreds of people on the street, near the corner of 145th Street. I knew there was a liquor store near where the greatest activity was, and as I got closer, I realized that they were looting the store. Feeling somewhat alone and helpless as I noticed that no other police presence was visible, I determined that I just had to continue to walk toward the looting mob. I didn't feel too happy about it, but I had no other choice since I was in uniform. When I got within fifty yards of the looters, they stopped when they saw me approaching. They must have thought I had about 100 paratroopers amassed on a roof top, ready to descend at my hand signal. It surely couldn't have been because of one lonely five-foot-eight and one-half inch white-haired police captain. I was beginning to think that the whole mob would disband and I would saunter into the subway without incident – sort of like Moses parting the Red Sea. No such luck. As soon as the looters realized I was strictly alone, they went back to passing the booze out of the store to the many waiting, eager hands.

I had to say something, so I said as I walked by, "Save a quart of Johnny Walker Black for me, champ." One of the looters replied, "You got two, Captain." Whereupon they made way for me and I was able to continue on my way to the subway entrance. When I got downstairs, I again found the stairs in total darkness, so I again went through the routine of lighting matches with my left hand while keeping my right hand on my revolver, gripped more tightly this time. Again, the gate was locked and the whole area in darkness. I climbed back up the stairs and walked to the nearest public phone I could find, which happened to be three blocks away at 148th Street. I was surprised to find the phone still operational. I called the 30th precinct and spoke to the desk lieutenant, who happened to be a relative of mine.

"Freddy, this is Pep. I'm on the corner of 148th Street and St. Nick. Can you send a radio car to pick me up?"

"What the hell are you doing there, Pep? Are you nuts?"

"Freddy, I'm trying to get into the subway, which is locked, and I'm standing here in uniform, so I'm not too popular. By the way Fred, send some troops to 145th and St. Nick – they are ripping off the liquor store."

Freddy said, "OK, Pep, the troops and the radio car are on the way."

"Thanks Fred, I owe you one. See you later."

The car picked me up within moments and drove me to the 30th precinct while the other cars responded to the looting condition at 145th Street to break up that party. I found out when I saw the lieutenant at the "30" that looting was rampant in the precinct and throughout the city. I thanked him for rescuing me with his troops, used his phone to call District 3, and left word for them to have someone open the gate for me at 146th Street so the damn commanding officer could get to his command! Three officers were waiting for me when I got to 146th Street with emergency lanterns in their hands.

"Sorry, Cap, we didn't know you were trying to get in."

"It's OK guys. I hope the coffee is on."

They replied, "No luck, Cap, no power." I could see it was going to be one of those nights – and it was!

The action never stopped. Looting and robberies were going on all over on city streets. The subways, then, were the safest place in town because they were closed! The transit police job consisted mainly of preventing people from entering the system since there was no power to provide service. Preventing damage to the transit system became our main concern. However, many of us became involved in street conditions since we couldn't ignore what was happening on the streets. We also knew that our brother officers on the street force had their hands full and needed help. In fact, after a few hours of continued street lootings, we were assigned to street conditions. My command was given 135th Street, 125th Street, and 116th Street on Lenox Avenue to safeguard. We did a good job, too, making several arrests and had restored order by morning at those locations. I was on patrol in a radio car throughout the whole night. It was like a scene from World War II. We would chase a mob from looting one store, only to find another mob looting another store right across the street. We'd chase them only to see another group hit another store a half-block away and so, off we'd go in hot pursuit. We would drive up sidewalks and over broken glass; jump out of the car, swinging our sticks and grabbing whom we could, run the culprits over to the precincts, and then get back to patrol. And so it went throughout the night.

By dawn, it was just about over, and as we went for coffee, I couldn't help feeling sorry for the sanitation department and the store owners with all those broken windows, doors, and lost merchandise. I went back to the district to do the necessary paperwork and await orders from headquarters. I held over some of the men and advised those going home to get some sleep because I'd probably have to call them in again the next night if the blackout continued. I worked until 2:00 p.m. and then decided to go home for a few hours sleep and to take a fresh shower. The bed never felt as good as it did that day! I set the alarm for 6:00 p.m. and fell fast asleep. I jumped up three hours later when the alarm went off, took another shower, shaved, got dressed, had a good dinner, kissed Eileen goodbye, and headed back to the "Big Three House" for another night in the trenches. It was a whole different scene this time. No crowds roaming around looting. Plenty of police presence everywhere, stores boarded up, and surprisingly, most of the debris cleaned up. I felt better as I entered the subway, where I had no trouble getting in. I was on duty only about two hours when the regular lights went on, announcing that the power was restored and the "blackout" was over.

By midnight, things were back to normal – normal operations and conditions prevailed. I released all the men working extra duty after thanking them all for the professional way they responded to the needs of the city under very trying conditions. I added that I was proud of every one of them and that it was another example of the excellent work done in the "Big Three House." I went off duty myself and felt very good during the drive home. I knew it would still take the city a few more days to really get back to normal, but at least we could see the light at the end of the tunnel. In retrospect, the prior "blackout" had almost been a fun thing with very little looting, lots of goodwill shown with people looking out for one another, some romantic episodes, many serious drinking bouts, and some monetary losses. But that was about it. This time it sure was different. I hope it never happens again!

Before concluding my account of what happened in District 3 while I was in command, I want to cite just a few of the outstanding police actions by my officers. I hope all District 3 members recognize that I'm citing them all when I cite just a few of the notable cases.

1. PO Keyer, in the dead of winter, dove into the icy waters of the Harlem River to rescue a drowning female. He was awarded the Department's Medal of Honor.

2. POs Healey and Kaica arrested a culprit who had brutally beaten an airline stewardess at the 96th Street IND station, and then pushed her in front of an approaching subway train. As a result of these two officers searching the immediate vicinity with the victim in their radio car, the culprit was apprehended at the victim's apartment. He had the gall to go there after finding her keys in the stolen pocketbook, along with her personal papers and her address. This

same culprit was subsequently identified for another brutal attack on a woman at the 155th Street IND subway station. He was also identified as the individual responsible for other brutal crimes against women.

3. Sgt. Maurice and POs Di Gregorio, Patterson, and Wager were involved in a high-speed chase where eleven shots were fired at the officers by armed robbers fleeing from a grocery store holdup. The officers gave chase in two radio cars and the culprits were arrested after they rammed one of the radio cars, totaling the car and seriously injuring two of the officers.

4. A number of violent crimes against elderly females were being committed at the 190th Street IND subway station and in Fort Tryon Park, immediately adjacent to the station. A stakeout was set up and surveillance conducted by multiple anti-crime and plainclothes units. These assignments lasted approximately three months and resulted in the apprehension, positive identification, arrest, and conviction of the individual responsible for these crimes. The 34th Precinct of the City Police Department worked very closely with us on this stakeout and assisted us materially in breaking the case.

5. The attempted murder of a railroad clerk took place at the 148th Street subway station on September 7th, 1978. PO Massey, a member of the uniformed force

assigned to plainclothes, had worked a late tour on that date and felt he could develop information through informants that would aid the department in apprehending the culprits. He was placed on special assignment and on September 14th, 1978, after a week long investigation and stakeout of the area, two suspects were arrested for the crime. PO Massey's information and undercover role played a major part in breaking the case.

6. Apprehension of two suspects for two homicides, four robberies, and two attempted murders at the Lenox Avenue and 148th Street IRT subway on March 30th, 1978. Although the actual arrests were made by our Detective Division, personnel from District 3's anti-crime unit – Sgt. Casey and POs Koratzanis, Castro and Alayon -- played a major role in catching these two violent criminals. Front page coverage was given the arrest by the newspapers, and it was also carried by the radio and television stations. The very laws governing juvenile violent crime procedures were changed in the State of New York as a direct result of this arrest. In fact, Governor Carey became personally involved and was instrumental in effecting the necessary changes.

7. Sgt. Birbiglia, aided by POs Hernandez, Alayon, Castro, and Devine arrested seven suspects who were conducting an illegal gambling operation at the 181st Street IRT subway station. Proceeds were

estimated to be one million annually.

I think you will agree that the members of District 3 were very effective in discharging their duties! While I was serving as the commanding officer of District 3, my old detective partner, Jim Rooney, retired. And when he did, a part of me retired also. Jim had been my PBA vice president and succeeded me as PBA president. Jim was so much a part of the department and had done so much for his fellow officers. He left a void that can never be filled.

Sometime in September 1978, I became increasingly aware of a conflict developing between the borough chief and myself regarding command discipline. Each of us had directly opposite viewpoints on that subject. I have already expressed my viewpoint, so there is no need to restate it again. The borough chief disagreed with me, and in all fairness to him, he gave me many opportunities to alter my views. We even had several conversations on the subject, and after some debate, he usually honored my recommendations. But we didn't change each other's views. Eventually, I was transferred from the "Big Three House" due to such differences.

I said goodbye to the troops at six consecutive roll calls, thanked them for the great job they had done, told them how proud I was to have had the honor of being their commanding officer for those exciting eighteen months, wished them all luck, and started into my office to remove my belongings. The men snapped to attention and then gave me a standing ovation that lasted a full five minutes. After which, each officer entered my office to shake my hand, each one telling me how much they enjoyed working for me, and all of them wishing me the best of luck. It was a very emotional scene. I hated walking out of the "Big Three House," but the men made it easier to do by the respect they had shown me. I said my final goodbyes on the way out, went upstairs, got into my car, and drove home – feeling so empty.

One final comment on the "Big Three House" -- A few months after my transfer to the Operations Unit, I received a call from one of the members of District 3 asking me to drop by the command the next afternoon to address the third platoon roll call. I agreed to do so, and the next day, I showed up there as requested. When I entered the district, I was met with a rousing cheer and loud applause. I soon discovered the true reason why they wanted me there. The troops were called to attention at roll call, whereupon I was presented with a beautiful gold pocket watch and a handsome plaque. The plaque was engraved as follows:

Presented to
CAPTAIN JOHN MARTIN
In appreciation for your THOUGHTFULNESS,
CONSIDERATION, AND KINDNESS for the men
in your COMMAND
WE WILL MISS YOU AND YOU WILL ALWAYS
BE REMEMBERED
THE MEMBERS OF DISTRICT 3 – 1979

In making the presentations, one of the officers re-marked that they were going to get me a set of handmade golf woods, but they found out from talking to my wife that I was just a "hacker." So, they decided on the watch instead. They were right – on both counts! I will certainly never forget the members of the "Big Three House" and their ex-pressions of respect and regard shown to me.

Chapter 20

My next assignment was to the Operations Unit, the communications hub and nerve center of the department. I was placed in Squad F-3, which meant I worked from 3:00 p.m. to 11:00 p.m. steady with Fridays and Saturdays off. I had never worked in Operations before, so at least it would be a new experience – even for an old-timer like me. I just didn't like the idea of being so close to the "big brass" since we didn't exactly get along too well. But what the hell – the pay was the same and at least I knew a lot of the old-time sergeants working there. They would show me the ropes in a hurry. Besides, my boss was a friend of mine and a guy for whom I had great respect. After a few hours in the O/U, I began to better understand and appreciate their function. And I began to realize how efficiently they operated under all kinds of stressful situations.

The guys were mainly a very happy group, always coming up with fantastic comical remarks under all kinds of trying conditions. This annoyed me at first, until I realized that they never missed a beat. I mean, they really had their fingers on the pulse of things. They always seemed to take the proper action to get the job done effectively, in the shortest possible time and all the while, they'd be making these crazy comments. They asked questions like, "Fred Astaire had three dancing partners who won Oscars. Who were they?" Or, "What was Hoot Gibson's horse named?" Things like that. Or the story one of the sergeants told me when he was in the Service and stationed somewhere down South. "Sgt. Joe" was of Italian extraction, born in the "Hell's Kitchen" section of Manhattan. Even though "Hell's Kitchen" is located only a few blocks west of the theatre district, to the people living there, it is light years away. Anyway, maybe that's where Sgt. Joe got his acting ability from, for he was some actor. Well, while stationed down South during World War II, Joe had an Army buddy who was a Southerner whose folks lived on a farm near the camp. So one night, Joe and his buddy were riding along this old dirt road in the guy's car. It was about 2:00 a.m. when the guy stopped the car, got out, and started throwing pebbles at the upstairs window. Joe thought his friend had gone crackers, when the window opened and an elderly guy with a stocking cap on his head inquired while fighting through a yawn, "Who the hell is it?"

Joe's buddy answered, "It's me, Pa!"

"I'll be right down, son," said the old timer. After which he led the two soldiers into the kitchen where Joe's friend's mother was already making coffee. Everything was going along fine with Joe entertaining them with his stories of life in the "Big Apple" when he realized that the old timer was standing directly behind him, peering at the back of his head.

The old guy suddenly exclaimed to his wife and son, "He's got pink ears in back, just like us!" Joe ended his story by commenting, "Imagine that my buddy brought me to his house just so his folks could see what an Italian guy looked like!" They had never seen one before! I'm sure Joe charmed them so much during his visit that Italians became their favorite people – besides Southerners, of course.

Joe weaved that little story during a five-minute coffee break one night. It's just an example of how the guys made it easier to get through the tours at the Operations Unit. As I said earlier, it is a very busy place, being the "clearing house" of the department. Actually, about 95% of all the calls requiring transit police attention would come through the Operations Unit. Whether it be a fire somewhere in the system, a train derailment, a blackout, a sick or injured person, report of a crime, a flood, a missing person, a lost child, a person jumping in front of a train, or whatever – it usually comes through the Operations Unit first. Time flies rapidly in there and before you know it, your tour is over and you leave there thinking about man's inhumanity to man. You know, just from what came in on your tour, you realize it's a pretty grim world out there. And just when you are about to become a confirmed cynic, you remember some details from when you were the CO of the "Big Three House," – about how someone returned found money to the individual who lost it, or about a black Muslim who ripped off his turban and wrapped it around a police officer's wounded leg after he was shot – and you begin to see some hope. Maybe not much, but some!

I wish I could do a better job of conveying how effectively these guys in operations function under stressful conditions. I'll try by describing one of the scenes in the O/U when a "caper" goes down. It goes something like this. A police officer answers the phone,

Officer Smith: This is PO Smith, may I help you?
Concerned Citizen: Yes, I'm a concerned citizen and I want to report that a transit authority bus just went out of control and rammed into a one-story frame house at 120th Street & Linden Blvd.
Officer Smith: Is anyone hurt?
Concerned Citizen: How the hell do I know? I'm just reporting it.
Officer Smith: Thank you very much, sir.
Concerned Citizen: You'll take care of it?
Officer Smith: Yes, may I have your name sir?
Concerned Citizen: No, I did my duty, I called.

And then the concerned citizen hangs up. Officer Smith then proceeds to shout to everyone within earshot,

Officer Smith: A TA bus just ran into a private house at

> 120th Street & Linden Blvd. Get the District 20 radio car with supervision to respond forthwith.

Radio Console Officer: RMP 201.

RMP 201: 201, go.

Radio Console Officer: Respond to 120th Street & Linden Blvd. regarding a TA bus that struck a one-story house. Do you have a supervisor in the car?

RMP 201: 201, negative, he's on foot patrol.

Radio Console Officer: 10-4, proceed to that location, an ambulance is on the way.

RMP 201: 201, 10-4, ETA is fifteen minutes.

Radio Console Officer: 10-4

Operations Captain: Notify the duty captain to respond to the scene. Notify the detectives to respond and investigate. Contact the bus division and notify them of the accident and request that they get their tow truck crew to the scene. Notify the legal bureau, then the chief and deputy chief, and any inspectors currently working of the condition. Also contact the chief executive officer of the Transit Authority and TA public relations.

Desk Sergeant: Also notify our emergency rescue units to respond to the condition, and get the damn paperwork started, you guys!

Which meant immediately an action memo was prepared, a "special or unusual occurrence" report developed,
and blotter entries and item record book entries made. The
radio console operator was kept busy communicating with
the cars dispatched, plus all other department vehicles with
their various and sundry other jobs going down at the same
time. The guys in the field were fighting their way through
the evening rush hour traffic to get to the scene of the accident, and the ambulance crew was struggling to get to the
house. The bus division tow truck was doing the same thing.
What about the poor occupants of the rammed house? And
the poor bus driver and his passengers? They were all caught
up in the drama that happened in the flick of an eye.

Pretty soon, reports started coming in from the field
units.

Duty Captain: This is the duty captain and here's the story.
The bus was crossing the intersection with
the green light in its favor when this truck,
license plate ABC, made an illegal right turn,
striking the right front side of the bus and
causing the bus driver to lose control -- the
bus then rammed into the side of the house.
The front four feet of the bus broke through
the outer brick wall of the kitchen destroying
the cabinets, dishwasher, oven, and the entire
front wall. The occupants of the house, Mr.
and Mrs. Jones, were having dinner at the

time and fortunately for them, they received only minor injuries and are en route to the hospital for treatment. The bus driver was the only one injured on the bus and he is also being treated for minor injuries at the same hospital. The driver of the truck is uninjured and was issued a summons for making an illegal turn and running a red light. The damaged bus has been removed after photos of the bus, truck, house, and the intersection had been taken by Detective Thomas. The condition is normal at this time.

Radio Console Officer: 10-4, Captain. Is District 20 doing the UOR?

Duty Captain: That's a 10-4. I'm resuming patrol.

Radio Console Officer: 10-4, Cap.

That ended that caper. Then the phone rang and it was the beginning of the next one. And that is how it always is at the Operations Unit.

Unfortunately, my assignment in the Operations Unit lasted only a month and a half, after which I was transferred, back to patrol duty. My boss and friend, Deputy Inspector "J.F." was also transferred to patrol duty. We were assigned to different patrol areas, so therefore, we didn't have much contact on the job. And our golf dates seemed to get harder to arrange because of the different tours, so we haven't seen each other much since our transfers. We both miss the

Operations Unit, along with our friend Captain Johnny "D" who is now the commanding officer of the O/U, and a good choice! We both miss all of the good guys still working there and those funny stories told by everyone assigned there.

The reason both the inspector and I were transferred from the O/U to patrol became necessary when the mayor of the city ordered all available members of the Transit Police Department to uniform patrol duties. Mayor Koch also ordered the city police to perform subway duty on an overtime basis. Such measures became necessary as a result of the multitude of violent crimes in the subways, including several murders. The mayor directed that a police officer be on board every subway train and most subway stations during the hours of 6:00 p.m. to 2:30 a.m. daily. The major posture of the department became one of police omnipresence, with uniformed officers highly visible in order to drastically reduce crime and make the subways safe for people. The mayor clearly demonstrated to everyone that the tremendous cost of police manpower was not a factor to be weighed against winning the war against subway crime. After all, a dollar value cannot be placed on the loss of a single life or the suffering and injuries sustained by crime victims and their families -- or for that matter, the sufferings of family members of the culprits. Mayor Koch deserves credit for the forthright manner with which he coped with the subway crime problem. And he has continued these massive police efforts for approximately eight months now, without any let up in sight. I recall that someone famous once said, "The more things change, the more they remain the same." Remember, back in 1965, the same problem of violent crime in the subways surfaced and Mayor Wagner ordered both transit and city police to cover every train and station during the hours of 8:00 p.m. to 4:00 a.m. daily. Mayor Wagner also tripled the size of the Transit Police Department to over 3,700 members to further cope with the problem of violent subway crime. Now, some fourteen years later, we are faced with same dilemma! What happened in those fourteen years, and why?

Chapter 21

After Mayor Wagner in 1965 tripled the size of the Transit Police Department to a sworn force of over 3,700 police officers, subway crime was reduced by a whopping 64%! There was virtually no crime during the hours of 8:00 p.m. to 4:00 a.m., and crimes reported during the other sixteen hours of the day were also very low. This trend continued for several months, very probably because the criminal element realized that the opportunity to commit successful crimes in the subways was limited – particularly during the night and early morning hours when the major part of the force was deployed. However, eventually the criminals recognized that most of the cops were assigned to the night hours and so, the opportunity to commit successful crimes must be between 4:00 a.m. and 8:00 p.m. They were right! And it wasn't long before department records indicated rapidly rising crime rates in those other sixteen hours.

The problem was that nothing of a concrete nature to combat such a rise in crime was being done, and I'm not exactly certain why. Perhaps the brass felt that the commitment of placing a police officer on every train and station during the hours of 8:00 p.m. to 4:00 a.m. was a political dictate from City Hall and could not be altered. Perhaps the brass thought the increase in crime during the other sixteen hours was a temporary one, and therefore, didn't want to risk a drastic shift of manpower only to have a sudden crime increase in the "taboo hours" of 8:00 p.m. to 4:00 a.m. Regardless, manpower deployment changes should have been made. They weren't, and crime skyrocketed. The subways were again unsafe and dramatic changes were in order.

The man who had the sense, and the courage, to order the necessary manpower deployment changes into the high crime hours was Sanford D. Garelik, then chief of the Transit Police Department. Chief Garelik made these changes after studying the subway crime trends, and after conferring with his district field commanders, all of whom wholeheartedly supported such changes. All of us had input concerning how such changes should be made and as a result, the model district concept was put into effect. The commanding officers of the "model districts" were given full authority and responsibility for running their commands. The department provided a redeployment of manpower allocation with complete authority to reassign members to squads and duty squads as needed. I was the commanding officer of the first model district at District 11, so I remember that the big change we made at the time was the redeployment of 72%

of the police officers from the tactical force unit that worked steady 4:00 p.m. to 8:00 a.m. hours. That was the key factor which immediately resulted in vastly improved coverage – visual and covert – during the <u>new</u> crime hours. It had been clearly determined that the new crime hours were now between 8:00 a.m. and 11:00 p.m. So that became the period during which our manpower deployment was heaviest.

The overall results indicated much success in coping with emerging crime conditions. Open felony complaints dropped dramatically and these crime reduction successes continued for several years since every command had been decentralized. Each district commander now had full authority and responsibility – you can't have one without the other – to deploy manpower to meet emerging crime conditions. Department morale soared, the troops broke their shoes to do the job, and excellent results were obtained. We really developed a police force of experienced, crime fighting officers who became expert in every facet of police operations. In very short order, the men became proficient at making all kinds of arrests, taking fingerprints, presenting court cases, conducting stakeouts, handling homicide cases, undertaking bookmaking and gambling cases, accepting anti-crime assignments and employing the tactics needed with those assignments, providing effective bus condition coverage, and enforcing traffic regulations that affect the hundreds of miles of city owned and operated bus routes. What a job the department was doing! I had never seen morale so high in my twenty-nine-plus years of service.

Unfortunately, the high morale and department effectiveness started to slide downhill after a three-year effort, not too rapidly at first, so it took a while for the signs to surface, but it was there. And it should have been coped with effectively and it wasn't. Why it wasn't dealt with effectively is something that still bothers me today. At the risk of "Monday morning quarterbacking," I can only state what I would have done to cope with the problem had I been chief. I would have:

- Promoted personnel to all ranks when vacancies occurred – as other uniform forces typically do.
- Permitted a certain percentage of paid overtime when crime conditions dictated it.
- Obtained a sufficient amount of radio patrol cars – in good condition – to effectively provide fast police response and improved patrol capability.
- Obtained lightweight scooters to use at certain times, and at certain subway stations and bus routes, to improve patrol effectiveness.
- Provided police protection for the bus riding public and the bus drivers.
- Provided the same police radio frequencies for all three police forces – city, housing, and transit.
- Redeployed manpower consistent with what crime statistics were telling us.
- Requested that the transit police force quota be increased to 4,000 members.

Since very few of these actions were instituted in any meaningful way, we are again back to square one! The entire force has been placed on ordered overtime, which costs millions of dollars. Part of the city police force has been placed on ordered overtime to perform subway duty, again costing millions of dollars. We still don't have the same radio frequencies, so the value of city police on subway duty is limited at best. Our department strength has been reduced to about 2,700 members, and we no longer have the manpower capability to provide adequate police protection on a sustained, continuing basis. It is ludicrous to expect department members to perform effectively on ordered overtime for such an extended period of time. Remember, police officers are also human. They have families, hobbies, need time off, have family issues to deal with, seek promotional opportunities, and need proper equipment to do the job. In spite of these basic needs, most cops like their jobs more than most people do, and that is something very special to build upon. It's the responsibility of those in authority to address those basic needs. If those in authority fail the police, they fail society. And without an effective police force, there is no society -- but rather, a mere jungle.

A really amazing thing happened the very day I had completed writing this section of the book. The next days' newspapers carried the headlines and excerpts from articles cited below. I believe these articles support the very points I am attempting to make in this story – almost as if I had written them myself. At least others are aware of the problem and are on top of it. Can we dare hope?

Daily News, August 29, 1979
More cops, more subway crime

Subway felony crime skyrocketed last week and reached a level almost equal to that at the height of the subway crime crisis despite increased patrols ordered by Mayor Koch, Transit Authority police reported yesterday.

In its weekly progress report to the mayor, TA police said that 251 felony crimes were reported, just 10 short of the number listed in the so-called "base week" of March 12.

And, despite the increased police patrols, over the last 23 weeks which cost the city $350,000 per week in overtime, there were less arrests last week – 127 – than in the base week, 159.

– Richard Edmonds

Daily News, August 30, 1979
Koch: will keep fighting war on crime in subway
By Richard Edmonds

Conceding defeat so far in the six-month war on subway crime, Mayor Koch declared yesterday: "Obviously, what we have done is not enough."

Despite a $350,000-per-week effort to post a uniformed cop

on virtually every train and station platform at night, the arrest rate of subway felons has remained relatively the same while violent crimes have steadily increased since the crackdown began last March.

Deputy Transit Police Chief Anthony Bouza reported to Koch on Tuesday that subway crime had reached a peak last week equal to the worst levels before the mayor launched his crackdown early last March.

"It is disturbing to see crime going up again in the subways, notwithstanding the enormous effort we have made in money and personnel," Koch said yesterday. "We will have to find additional techniques. The subways are the very arteries and veins of this city and must be given special attention."

A meeting on the problem

City Hall and transit police brass reportedly had noticed the trend over the last 23 weeks. Last week, Transit Police Chief Sanford Garelik and ranking members of his uniformed force attended a meeting with representatives of Deputy Mayor Herbert Sturz, Koch's strategist in the subway crime war.

At the meeting, all agreed that the increased patrols were too rigid and that most of the police force was deployed between the hours of 6 p.m. and 2 a.m.

In the last week, violent crime in the subway skyrocketed 48%, with 251 reported felonies. The number was only 10 less than the figure for the week of March 12, the "base week" before Koch ordered the crackdown.

Above ground, the New York Police Department also reported that all violent crime except rape had increased over the same period last year. Total crimes against persons were up 7.91% in the first four months of this year.

New York Post, Wednesday, August 29, 1979
Subway crime soars – Koch calls it 'awful'
By Randy Smith

MAYOR Koch said today he's "very concerned" about the soaring subway crime rate – which shot up 48 per cent last week to its worst level in six months.

Koch called the latest numbers "awful," and said he would ask his criminal justice coordinator, Herb Sturz, "to look into the matter and hopefully improve the situation."

But Sturz was on vacation in Martha's Vineyard, and Transit Police Chief Sanford Garelik was in Montreal for a conference of the American Public Transit Assn.

An aide said Sturz has already begun to redesign the overtime plan for fighting subway crime, which now costs the city

$350,000 a week, but refused to provide details until Koch gets them.

With Garelik away, Koch got the bad news from Deputy TA Police Chief Anthony Bouza.

The statistics showed that in the 23rd week of Koch's war on subway crime, felony reports jumped from 169 to 251.

That's only 10 short of the total for the last week the mayor beefed up car and platform patrols last March 19 in the face of a subway crime wave.

Thefts including 20 more necklace snatchings and 13 more drunk rollings accounted for most of the rise, with no rapes or murders reported in the week that ended last Sunday.

While arrest also rose 48 per cent from 86 to 127, they lagged far behind the 157 arrests notched in the base week.

A spokesman for Garelik said transit cops are still riding every train from 6 p.m. to 2 a.m., and city cops are still patroling most stations from 4 p.m. to 2 a.m.

"It's just one week," said the spokesman, Ed Silverfarb. "It's not really enough to draw any conclusions from."

A dozen plainclothes and decoy cops were added in the last

month, which Silverfarb said might explain the increased arrest totals.

Koch cut the plainclothes force by almost three-fourths when he beefed up the night shift from 300 uniformed and 200 plainclothes cops to a combined force of 900 transit and New York City police, all in uniform.

Koch also hired 68 new TA cops, and gave free bus and subway rides to all police, Housing Authority, correction and court officers, in uniform or not.

In the first week of Koch's war on subway crime, felony reports declined dramatically from 261 to 157. They have since ranged from a low of 137 in week number three to a high of 203 in week nineteen.

A total of 2082 TA cops, or five-sixths of the whole force, worked overtime last week. The total bill came to $198,861. City cops also get $150,000 a week in extra overtime to fight Koch's war.

As you can see from these newspaper articles, approximately $0.5 million dollars per week is being spent on overtime payments to police officers of both the Transit Police and City Police Departments to cope with the battle of subway crime. And we are <u>not</u> winning that battle! Why? Because,

- When emergency conditions continue for more than thirty days, the strain on the men shows and they begin to lose peak effectiveness.
- Many of the officers are being forced to work these overtime tours, so they are not properly self-motivated.
- Some officers effect minor arrests or are required by circumstances to issue a summons. Both of these procedures force the officers off patrol, and their posts are doubled up and assigned to some other officer. Thus, the vacated officer's post is covered, but only on paper. Patrol strength is thereby weakened, and the vicious culprits strike.
- There are no two-man patrols on the subway system and many of the subway stations are located in extremely high crime areas. Common sense dictates two-man patrols in these areas. Two officers so assigned would more than double their effectiveness as the criminals would be less apt to commit crimes at those locations. Additionally, the safety of the officers so assigned would be improved and the cost would be less than the cost incurred by one seriously injured or dead police officer. *Some police experts might argue differently here, suggesting that two man patrols could weaken both officers' effectiveness. I argue that here in the Big Apple, on a high crime post, both officers would fully realize that their effectiveness, and their lives, depended on each other.*

- Manpower deployment is again pretty much locked in to fixed hours with city police working from 6:00 p.m. to 2:30 a.m. Such fixed deployment is wrong, not because I say so, but because history, facts, and circumstances tell us it is wrong to remain so static. We must be flexible and innovative to meet emerging conditions. The bad guys are!

What the hell is wrong with us? First of all, these <u>supposedly</u> high crime hours are the wrong hours for making prudent and effective police assignments. Why? Because at 4:00 p.m., when the city police start their subway tours, school conditions have ended and the evening rush hour is just starting. This means huge crowds returning home from work on weekdays, and when you have large crowds entering and leaving the transit system, you generally <u>don't</u> have violent crimes. The type of crime you do have is of a surreptitious nature, grand larceny such as a pickpocket or a "bag opener." These types of crimes are not effectively prevented by the mere presence of one uniformed officer standing somewhere on a single subway platform or mezzanine! That uniformed officer would be much more effective as a crime deterrent on that same platform **AFTER** the rush hour crowds have thinned out. The officer then stands out as a "beacon of security" for all to see, and is in a position to properly observe conditions.

Other actions that should be taken:

- The city and transit police should be assigned to

more realistic crime fighting hours, starting at 7:00 p.m. until 3:30 a.m., where their presence would be seen and their effectiveness felt.

- The city police should also install one of their radio consoles, manned by one of their members, at the transit police operations unit so that instant police communications are maintained and coordinated by both police agencies – not a big deal, just a sensible one.

- Radio patrol cars of both departments should be manned by two officers, one from each department, and each equipped with his department's portable radios. In that way, contact is maintained by both departments concerning police conditions in the officers' assigned areas.

- Both city police and transit police should be required to ride trains, and by the interchange of both departments' portable radios and use of a city police radio console at the transit police operations unit, interdepartmental communications would be effectively maintained and public safety improved.

- Allocate overtime resources dynamically, alternating assignment periods and revisiting those allocations frequently based on periodic reviews of crime statistics.

Chapter 21

After my transfer from the Operations Unit, I decided to confer with my good friend, Father Jolley, founder and pastor of St. Columba's Roman Catholic Church in Brooklyn. I have known Father Ted, as he is called by his family and friends, for about twelve years. He is a wonderful priest, a great guy, and a good golfer – pretty much an unbeatable combination! He is aptly named since he is truly a jolly individual. We have a little thing going between us every time we get together. It goes like this. "Good evening, Monsignor." "Good evening, Inspector." Neither one of us will probably ever be promoted, but it's a little thing we do for each other's ego.

When I spoke to Father Ted about my latest transfer, I said, "What do you think, Father – are they trying to tell me something? Should I pack the job in?"

Father replied, "Some of the very top brass probably would be delighted if you packed it in, but the troops wouldn't." He added, "Why should you quit now, John – it's your job. You took all the examinations for all the ranks in the transit police. You belong there. Think of your family and don't retire until <u>you</u> are ready. Besides, you have to make inspector so I can drop your name when I'm playing a round of golf with some of my many police friends."

"Don't forget to tell them I'm from TRANSIT, Father. That thought alone will add a few strokes to their game! Meanwhile, I'll see what I can do with the bishop about getting you made Monsignor. See you Sunday night at your sister's house for a friendly game of cards." And I did, on many an occasion before and since our visit.

My story about the Transit Police Department would not be complete without mentioning, and thus paying tribute, to the four valiant police officers who were shot and killed in the line of duty. All four killings took place during the past decade or so.

Incident

Police Officer Innes, who was shot and killed while off duty and seated in his private car outside his home. He was killed by an individual he had arrested previously while on patrol on the subway, several years prior to the fatal incident. In the initial incident, Officer Innes was forced to draw his revolver and shoot the culprit several times, after the culprit had seized the officer's nightstick and repeatedly beat him over the head and body, inflicting serious injuries. The culprit recovered, although he was unable to function sexually as a result of his wounds. He was sent to prison for a period of time and after his release from prison, he sued the officer and the City of New York for a large sum of money. The culprit lost the case and I suppose he then began the plot to take Officer Innes's life. He discovered where the officer lived and began to harass and terrify the officer's family. He even exposed himself to the officer's children while shouting, "This is what your father did to me." Then he made obscene calls to the officer's wife. Finally, the reign of terror ended with the brutal slaying of Officer Innes. The department does not list Officer Innes's death as a line of duty incident. But they should, since he was killed as a direct result of his on-duty actions in shooting, and subsequently arresting, a dangerous individual.

Incident

Police Officer Michael Melchiona was shot and killed while on duty and assigned to uniform patrol in the vicinity of the 49th Street BMT subway station on February 28th, 1970. The officer had observed a male who appeared to be loitering in the Men's Room in the 49th Street subway station. Officer Melchiona was attempting to question the individual concerning his identity when the man suddenly seized the officer's service revolver and fled upstairs to the street. The unarmed officer pursued the culprit upstairs to the street and spotted him on 49th Street. 49th Street and Seventh Avenue is an extremely populated intersection, bordered by several theatres and many business establishments. By midafternoon, this area is teeming with people and those were the conditions that prevailed when the unarmed officer pursued his armed assailant into the crowded streets. People were scurrying left and right, panic- stricken at the sight of this unkempt individual walking the streets armed with a gun. Officer Melchiona closed within thirty feet of the culprit, who by then was directly across the street from him. The officer called to the man to drop the weapon and surrender. The culprit responded by firing one shot across the crowded street, striking the young officer in the heart. A city police officer on traffic duty then engaged in a blazing gun duel in which both the officer and the perpetrator were wounded. The suspect was arrested and eventually convicted of Officer Melchiona's murder. He had a long record of prior convictions for vicious crimes, and had been in and out of prison most of his adult life. Officer Melchiona was certainly not aware of his killer's background when he made his routine inquiries in the subway station. Just a good cop doing his job, for which he paid with his life.

Incident

Police Officer Sid Thompson was shot and killed while on anti-crime duty at the 174th Street & White Plains Road IRT elevated subway in the Bronx on June 5th, 1973. The officer was assigned that duty as a result of a series of passenger robberies in the area. At the subway station, Officer Thompson observed several males loitering and smoking cigarettes in the waiting room adjacent to the token booth. The officer approached the group and identified himself as a police officer while ordering them to put out their cigarettes.

Two of the group replied by whipping out automatic pistols and firing at the surprised officer, who was shot in the head and chest. Officer Thompson somehow managed to draw his revolver and fire several rounds at the suspects before he fell, mortally wounded. Two of the officer's rounds struck one of the fleeing culprits in the leg, enabling responding police to follow his bloody trail and make his subsequent arrest. The wounded perpetrator and his accomplices turned out to be notorious members of the Black Liberation Army and were wanted for killing other police officers in another city. Officer Sid Thompson's valiant actions were in the finest tradition of the Transit Police Department. Another good cop doing his job.

Incident

Police Officer John Skagen was shot and killed on June 28th, 1972 in the Hunt's Point IRT subway station while in civilian clothes, returning from court. I mentioned this tragic incident earlier in the book. John and I had become friends when I was the lieutenant-in-charge of the Firearms Training Unit and he was still on active duty in the Navy. He was only a cop for one year when he lost his life.

Subway crime continued to rise in 1978, and rose even more in the first few months of 1979. Despite the increase, nothing concrete was initially done to reverse the trend. More and more members of the department were retiring and they were not being replaced due to the fiscal condition of the city. The department still refused to permit members to work overtime, and so crime raged out of control. Eventually, Mayor Koch stepped in and took control of the Transit Police Department. He authorized and directed a total war on subway crime. Most of the officers of both police departments were ordered to perform overtime crime fighting tours in an effort to reduce subway crime.

The city newspapers reported constantly on the situation. Without their reporting, such a war on subway crime might not have been launched in the first place. The people of the City of New York owe them their gratitude for keeping the pressure on. Articles were being written almost daily in 1979, starting in March and continuing through October of that year. Sanford Garelik, the chief of the Transit Police Department at the time, was under constant scrutiny. Finally, in September 1979, Mayor Koch removed Sanford Garelik as chief of the Transit Police Department. The following excerpts from articles published in the *New York Post* and *Daily News*, tell some of the story.

New York Post
Wednesday, September 12, 1979

FIGHTING SUBWAY CRIME:
1. Unity is a logical first step
2. More manpower must be found
Mayor Koch's decision to unify the city's three separate

police forces under the direction of police commissioner Robert McGuire is a first and logical step toward their eventually complete integration.

It is meeting predictable resistance from the unions involved, and from some members of the Metropolitan Transit Authority. Yet it is surely the only sensible way of coping with the worsening crime that bedevils and frustrates this city.

To the Housing Police it is a "gimmick." To the TA police it is "public relations." The PBA fears manpower-starved precincts will be raided to provide cops for the subways or housing projects.

These are the natural responses of vested interests. But this is not a city of separate fiefdoms and it will survive as a totality or not at all.

Koch's move achieves the removal of controversial TA police chief Sanford Garelik. The exposure in *The Post* earlier this year of his distorted crime figures first revealed the extent of the subway crime wave and led the mayor to make himself personally responsible for its solution. Whether Garelik should be retained with his $49,000-a-year salary is an issue for debate but it should not divert anyone from the real issue.

That is still the subway crime wave. The heavy use of TA

police overtime has not resolved it. Indeed, over the last two weeks robberies and larcenies have increased.

Police integration is practicable and necessary. We cannot tolerate the rivalries or racial antagonisms which allegedly exist among the three services. They receive the same pay and pensions. They are targets for the same assailants.

The TA police claim a special expertise. City cops, they say, don't know the complex subway system, don't recognize the alarm signals of motormen sounding alerts and further, because of differences in equipment, once they enter the subway their radios go dead. It is for this reason, they note, that the 144 city cops now assigned to subway overtime can only be used on elevated stations.

These are excuses, not reasons. Cops should be able to go anywhere. They can be trained for any conditions, any situation, and be given the proper equipment.

The crucial answer to subway crime, however, is manpower. The TA force has been reduced by the fiscal crisis from 3200 patrolmen to 2400. There are pre-dawn periods, indeed, when less than 200 men are on the job. Allowing for leave and days off, the TA has only 1000 men to deploy on any one day.

But there are 450 stations and Koch's policy of guarding

them all, with concentrated forces between 6 p.m. and 2 a.m. – and two-man patrols at Times Square, 42nd Street and Eighth Avenue and West 4th Street – is being severely tested.

The present force, providing one cop for every 1300 passengers, is clearly inadequate. Our course is obvious. We can effectively challenge the subway crime wave only by restoring the TA force to its level of 1975, when it was one of the most efficient in the nation.

To hire another 1000 men would cost an extra $20 million a year. That must be a major consideration for the mayor. But his overtime plan is running at a cost of over $18 million a year, and there is no end in sight to the battle against subway violence.

The solution seems clear. Obviously Commissioner McGuire, short 8000 city cops, could be tempted to raid Peter to pay Paul. But, as the man now in charge of this city's overall security, he would do so at his peril, so long as subway crime is the primary aggression shadowing the city.

Daily News
Wednesday, September 12, 1979

Plots subway fight without city cops
By VINCENT LEE and RICHARD EDMONDS

Newly named Transit Police Chief James Meehan pledged yesterday to take a more flexible approach in the battle against violent subway crime, but said that city cops will not be regularly assigned to trains and stations underground.

Meehan also told the Daily News that he won't be bound by the rigid patrols that his predecessor instituted but often failed to deliver – the promise of a uniformed cop on every train and platform after dark.

Meehan, who replaced Sanford Garelik yesterday in a sweeping shakeup, took charge of the country's sixth largest police force yesterday in a reshuffling that was denounced by the city's three police unions.

City cops "have own problems"

In an interview in an office occupied until yesterday by deputy transit police chief Anthony Bouza, who also was ousted, Meehan said: "I spent this morning just trying to ascertain what the crime problems are ... whether strategies should remain in place or change. I see the possibility that we might change some of the strategies (for) a different mix in deployment." Meehan said, "I do not see city police being used in the subway. City police have their own problems trying to establish patrols throughout the city with limited, cutback manpower."

Meehan, former chief of personnel for the City Police Department, said that he told his family about his promotion within hours after he formally received the news Monday from police commissioner Robert McGuire.

"My son, Thomas, has been on the job as a cop since 1973. He asked me, 'Does this mean I'll be riding subways?'" Meehan said. He acknowledges that many other officers had expressed the same concern.

Meehan declared, however, that the City Police Department, the Transit Authority Police and the Housing Authority Police – now under the unified command of the police commissioner – should keep their "integrity." For the moment, Meehan said, he is looking into the sharing of training and management resources only...

Chapter 22

My tours of duty since my last transfer out of the Operations Unit continue to make life "on the job" interesting for me -- although I must admit, not nearly as interesting as when I had my own command. A duty captain's function just isn't as demanding or self-rewarding as that of a district commander. As a district commander, you take the job home with you. As a duty captain, you walk out the door after your tour is finished and you pretty much don't think about it again until you return for your next tour. Nevertheless, life can still be interesting for a duty captain.

Let me tell you about a few of the incidents I have worked on since being transferred to the "Rockaways," where we have a transit police district located in the heart of the Rockaways, on Beach 116th Street. I suspect the "big brass" hung me out to dry when they assigned me there. But I think the exposure to the salt air will actually preserve me a little longer. I hope so. At least the environment is different down here. However, even Rockaway has changed and we have plenty of subway crime here. Besides, our patrol area extends beyond Rockaway and includes some very high crime areas in Brooklyn.

The command complement is small in comparison to other department commands, and almost all of the men assigned here have high seniority, with the exception of the commanding captain. He is a comparatively young man, about thirty-seven years old, with a calm demeanor and a good head on his shoulders. He and I get along fine together and manage to keep out of each other's hair by working opposite tours. He leaves me a note in his locker (which he is kind enough to share with me) if he wants me to handle a particular matter. And I do the same for him, so we have very open lines of communication. He has been a captain as long as I have, being one of the guys I referred to as "The Whiz Kids" that I was so terrified of competing against when taking the captain's exam.

As I said, the rest of the command's complement consists of mostly senior members, including the lieutenants and the sergeants. I have worked with some of these guys in other commands in the past, so we are not strangers to each other. And that makes for a good working relationship. It's a competent command whose experienced members work hard combating crime in their assigned areas of patrol. I like the men and I enjoy their stories, comments, and remarks about their experiences on the job. "Cop stories" are still very much in vogue when you are on the job. And I'm now working on my second generation of cops!

Most of the conditions I have responded to since my

transfer have been pretty routine. Routine, that is, if you classify a bus driving through someone's kitchen wall as they are eating dinner as routine; or a blazing inferno engulfing the main train bridge to the Rockaways; or a few "Rock Concerts" by the boardwalk – not to mention the huge crowds going to the beach during the summer months.

I did respond to a peculiar incident that took place on August 13th, 1979. It occurred on the Long Island Expressway near Exit 48 at about 5:00 p.m. A couple of patrol officers from the command had finished a day tour and were carpooling together, driving home on the LIE. Traveling eastbound, one of the officers came up behind a yellow and wood-grained 1979 Omni four-door sedan, which was occupied by a male driver and a female passenger. Traffic at this point was heavy and slow and as the officer closed his vehicle to within about fifteen feet, he noticed a black revolver resting against the door on the driver's side, pointed in the direction of the officer's car. The gun was in the right hand of the driver and without any warning, he fired one round at the officer. The other officer, who had been dozing in the front passenger's seat, heard the gunfire, sat up and asked what had happened. "That guy in front just fired a shot at us." The officers pursued the Omni. Due to the traffic congestion, the Omni could not go too fast, but it did change lanes several times. Near Exit 49, just east of Route 110, the officers managed to pull alongside the Omni. They were in the left lane and the Omni was in the center lane. They called to the driver of the Omni, identifying themselves as police officers and displaying their shields. With the traffic moving slowly, they were able to pull their vehicle in front of the Omni, forcing it to stop in the right lane. Both officers got out of their car and were approaching the Omni when the driver fired another shot at them. Both officers then returned the fire, emptying their off-duty revolvers by firing at the vehicle. The female passenger jumped out of the car and the driver sped away, heading east on the Expressway. A state trooper in an unmarked car picked up one of the officers and they pursued the Omni. But they were unable to overtake the car and the driver managed to escape. Suffolk County Police Units responded to the scene, took sworn statements from the two transit police officers, and broadcast all necessary alarms to their patrol units. At about 10:00 p.m., the culprit was apprehended at his residence in Central Islip by two Suffolk County cops in the Street Crime Unit. The culprit was taken to the 2nd Precinct in Huntington, where he gave a statement admitting he fired three shots at the officers because he thought they were tailgating his car. He was booked on charges of attempted murder and held for the Suffolk County grand jury.

It was most fortunate that no one was injured or killed as a result of the gunfire on the LIE. Episodes like that can certainly cause a sudden increase in ridership on the LIRR!

Chapter 23

E ileen and I went on vacation starting February 21st, 1980 and ending on March 13th, 1980. We again visited Florida as was our custom for our usual "winter respite" which afforded us the opportunity to enjoy some Florida sunshine and escape the cold weather up North. We did not read any New York newspapers while we were away, so I was startled to learn that two of our police officers had been shot and killed in the performance of police duty. Another new crime wave had invaded the subways.

New police plans were formulated to meet the new challenge and as a result of those plans, I was transferred from Rockaway to Coney Island, where I became the commanding officer of District 34. I was happy to have a command again and hoped that I could chip off the rust of being "on the beach" for a full year without any command authority. Only time will tell if I can, but I intend to try!

A day before my transfer from the Rockaways to District 34, while still functioning as a duty captain, a shooting took place between an off-duty transit police officer and three stick-up men. Here's how the shooting went down. On March 11th, 1980 at about 8:00 p.m., one of our off-duty officers was food shopping in a small neighborhood super-market in Brooklyn. While weighing some fruit on a scale, he heard a voice say, "Give it up." Looking in the direction of the cashier, the officer observed two males with guns. One held a sawed-off shotgun aimed at the manager, and the other male held a pistol pointed at the cashier. The off-duty officer reached inside his jacket and attempted to draw his revolver, whereupon the male wielding the shotgun glanced quickly at the officer. However, the guy toting the shotgun turned his attention to the store manager in an ef-fort to force the manager to open the safe. At that moment, the officer pulled his revolver and fired six rounds, hitting the male with the shotgun at least twice. Despite being hit, the culprit stayed on his feet until overpowered by the of-ficer and the store manager. The male with the pistol fled to the rear of the store without exchanging any shots, where he joined up with a third culprit. Despite having an empty gun, the officer stationed himself at the front entrance to seal off what he thought was the culprits' only way out. But the two culprits escaped via a rear exit only to be picked up later based on information supplied by the officer.

The three individuals had committed more than fifty similar stick-ups in the area. Department policy requires a superior officer in the rank of captain or above to respond to all firearms discharges for the purposes of ascertaining if the officer's actions were necessary, legal, and within the department's guidelines. Not a simple task, but a necessary one. Let me explain why.

Immediately after any shooting, many units are directed to respond to the scene – patrolmen, detectives, ballistics, forensics, the assistant DA, the medical examiner (if deaths are involved), news reporters, PBA representatives, PBA lawyers, and police brass. Everyone has a job to do. The shooting scene is preserved, witnesses rounded up and questioned, physical evidence studied, etc. Naturally, the officer is subjected to a barrage of questions regarding the incident – Why were you there? What were your movements prior to the shooting? Were you drinking? Do you use narcotics? Was it necessary to shoot? Did you identify yourself as a police officer? (If he did, he would very probably be dead.) Describe how it happened <u>again</u>, from the very beginning. And so on and so on, and over and over again, until everyone connected with the investigation is satisfied that the shooting is not only legal and justified, it must also conform to the department's guidelines. Field reports must be correlated and prepared by the captain in charge, and forwarded forthwith to the chief's office for immediate review.

It is a rare day indeed when the chief is satisfied with the captain's initial report! The captain usually winds up being called at home and directed to resubmit additional reports requiring additional information before the chief is satisfied with the final results. So what – captains get paid pretty well, while the cop in the trenches with his life on the line gets paid a lot less. Many times, the cop wonders why he got involved in the first place. Thank God for all of us that they do!

Just a comment on the shooting incident described above. Certainly, the officer's actions were legal, necessary, and proper, and within the department's guidelines. The officer's actions were also highly courageous and reflected very well on the department. His actions also resulted in preventing a holdup, as well as possible deaths or injuries to a bunch of people. His efforts also led to the apprehension of three individuals suspected of committing over fifty such crimes. Not a bad night's work!

On March 13th, 1980, I was officially transferred. Looking back on my year-long assignment as a duty captain in the Rockaways, I cannot say that I enjoyed it that much due to the fact that my role was not a very active one. I felt that I had been "hung up on the beach" to dry out and perhaps, retire. Therefore, I eagerly accepted the new assignment in District 34 with vigor and renewed interest. I only hoped that I could chip off the rust and do the job the boss expected. I was sorry to leave the company of the members of District 23 in Rockaway, as they were all good cops and great companions.

Upon assuming command of District 34, I noticed the difference within myself of just how good it felt to be a part of a command again. The way the troops said, "Good morning, Captain," told a good part of the story. The respect was there, and now I had to maintain it! It took me a few weeks to acclimate myself to procedures and conditions within the confines of "The 34 House" since we covered such a vast geographical area: fifty-one stations on five different lines, and we were also responsible for transit police coverage of Staten Island – that lovely haven within the City of New York, separated by "The Narrows" of New York Harbor. In order to get there from Coney Island, it was necessary to drive over the Verrazano Bridge, a twenty-five minute drive under the best of conditions. Fortunately, most of our police assignments to Staten Island were "paper ones," meaning we generally responded after a condition was reported since we did not have sufficient manpower to provide patrol coverage on a daily basis. We had our hands full trying to fight crime on the fifty-one subway stations in Brooklyn. Figuratively speaking, Staten Island was in a different world.

Still, I was frequently getting pressure from officials and community councils to provide transit police coverage to that borough. I resisted such pressure simply because priorities dictated otherwise. My troops would have loved any Staten Island assignment since many of them resided there. But hell, I wasn't running a popularity contest – I was running a very busy command in Brooklyn. Let me describe what running such a command was like. We'll use a question and answer approach, as if I was responding to a direct inquiry from the department brass. It goes something like this.

Question: Initially, upon your designation as commanding officer, what were the problems confronting this command? List in priority order, giving details and your resolutions of same.

Answer: The foremost problems confronting me as commanding officer of District 34 were high incidences of certain types of crimes, particularly during the second platoon hours. These crimes include necklace snatches, bag snatches, passenger robberies by youths, projectiles thrown at trains, criminal trespass, criminal mischief, and graffiti. I have attempted to resolve these crime problems by alerting the District 34 patrol force and supervisory personnel of existing conditions through roll call instructions, informal conferences, post condition cards, perusal of TP-67s, TP-4Es, and the use of devised crime statistics charts. I have also directed specific assignments of uniform, anti-crime, and plainclothes officers to cope with emerging crime conditions. In addition, I have requested and received assistance from CWPS and the Detective Division. Personnel assigned to this command are repeatedly alerted to prevent recurrence of crimes through diligent patrol. As a result, felony arrests are up 51% for the first six months of 1980. Despite the efforts and assignments indicated above, crime figures for this command continue to increase dramatically with a 40% increase in felony complaints for the first six months of the year. The 40% increase in felony complaints is offset somewhat by the 51% increase in felony arrests.

Question: Presently what are the problems confronting this command and what have been your attempts at solving them? List in priority order with details of your concomitant efforts.

Answer: Some of the present problems confronting this command are:

1. Increase in Crime

I study crime statistics every tour and direct specific roll call assignments to recent crime locations during times of occurrence. Such assignments include anti-crime units, plainclothes details, and uniform officers – in addition to special attention by the sector patrol cars.

Patrol members are made aware of crime conditions on their posts through roll call instructions and District 34 crime recap sheets. Additionally, all superior officers of this command are directed to make ongoing roll call assignments to meet emerging crime conditions in order to exact meaningful patrol performance from their subordinates.

Contact is maintained with the city police precinct commanders regarding matters of mutual concern, which results in coordinated police efforts. A clear example of such coordination is the deployment of men and tour hours of both city and transit police Coney Island summer squads. This coordination has permitted both police units to cope effectively with the huge crowds in the Coney Island area, particularly on weekends and holidays.

2. School Conditions

The volume of school conditions in this command exceeds all other district commands. In all, sixty school condition assignments are in effect every school day, pervading every section of the command's geographical area. Nine of the high schools, with a total enrollment of 154,000 students, are located within the immediate area adjacent to the D-M-F-B lines of the Rapid Transit System. Most of the students attending these schools enter and exit the transit system at the same or adjoining stations.

In addition to normal tensions and conflicts caused by natural school rivalries, additional tensions exist. These tensions have resulted in violent crimes on the stations and trains of the F line due to the large number of students from other areas of the borough that are forced to attend FDR High School. Incidents occur in the school and spill over onto the streets and continue onto the transit system. Procedures have been established among the various agencies concerned to effectively cope with the "FDR Problem." Liaison is thus maintained with the 66th Precinct, the Brooklyn South Task

Force, School Authorities, the District 34 commanding officer, District 34 superior officers, the two sergeants and 16 police officers that constitute the District 34 traffic control squad, and one sergeant and nineteen police officers from CWPS.

There is no doubt in my mind that a large percentage of crimes committed during the second platoon hours are committed by students attending schools in this area. Once a student is apprehended and convicted, stronger corrective action within the criminal justice system is needed to deal with those who commit violent or repeated felony crimes.

3. Reduction in Manpower

District 34 manpower has been steadily reduced from 147 police officers, 5 lieutenants and 11 sergeants to its present quota of 89 police officers, 4 lieutenants and 9 sergeants. Additionally, code 99 overtime has been reduced from 152 hours per day to 42 hours daily. Also, 26 city police assignments to 26 of the District 34 stations are no longer in effect.

In order to cope with this loss of district manpower, squad realignments were necessary to obtain better coverage and deployment during the hours of greatest need. Volunteers were obtained to fill voids on the first and fourth platoons, where more violent types of felony crime are likely to occur.

Question: Under your leadership, what improvements or changes have you effected as the commanding officer?

Answer: I have taken the following actions to improve our operations:

1. Realigned subordinate superior officers' duties and responsibilities, equalizing their respective workloads concerning administrative and patrol duties.

2. Published district directives and memos on such subjects as: roll call procedure changes to meet emerging field conditions, patrol procedures, presence of members in district office, utilization of R/D officers assigned, and patrol productivity procedures to ensure uniformity.

3. Strived to maintain channels of communication at all times, both up and down the chain of command, and I am always available to confer with members of the command.

4. Tested the knowledge of lieutenants, sergeants, and police officers as to existing conditions within the district.

5. Instructed subordinate superior officers to receive grievances, gripes, etc. from any member or representative of a line or other recognized department organization, and to take proper action when warranted, pending my approval.

6. Initiated improvements in the district muster area and desk officer area by: having the entire area painted; erecting two separate offices – one for the PAA (clerical) assigned and one for the detective squad members; relocated and reorganized bulletin boards and installed new hard board covers, clearly labeled and depicting such subjects as alarms, training bulletins, school conditions, wanted and missing persons, etc.

7. Personal patrol inspections of all areas of my command, both uniform and covert, are made by me to ensure that personnel assigned are performing their duties in a proper manner.

8. Designated additional parking facilities to make things a little easier for our members.

9. Instituted plainclothes assignments for specific conditions, such as "lush workers" on the RR line.

10. Changed the crime statistics charts and monthly crime reports formula consistent with current guidelines.

11. Obtained an additional sergeant with previous traffic control experience to help improve school condition situations.

12. Devised and published a "Command Profile" containing important command data and patrol procedures.

13. Instituted "concerted patrol" on posts 44 through 47 on the first and third platoons during the summer months.

14. Caused district train patrols to be revised to provide alternate special attention coverage to certain stations, such as West 8th Street D-F-M lines, the 86th Street N line, and the Bay 50th Street B line.

Question: What possible solutions are beyond your immediate control and require department, zone, or outside agency support?

Answer: Here are the things we need help with:

1. Additional police equipment such as: an additional RMP to cover another patrol sector; police lightweight scooters to provide rapid response and improved police visibility in certain areas and at select posts.

2. Increase in manpower and an increase in the number of train patrols during evening and early morning non-rush hours.

3. Mandatory limited sentences for those convicted of violent crimes and repeat offenders of other crimes against the person.

4. Utilization of existing but abandoned government facilities, such as the Brooklyn Navy Yard, Brooklyn Army Base, and Floyd Bennett Field, to be used as detention facilities for felons.

5. Use of auxiliary police units, if qualified, for certain duties such as train patrol, school conditions, and emergency medical assignments.

6. Additional "satellite" central booking and courts to reduce travel time and time lost from patrol.

Question: How do you gauge your subordinates' performance in preventing crime, apprehending violators, or providing other services?

Answer: I believe that high police visibility must be maintained through diligent patrol by uniform and anti-crime units working in conjunction with each other. This is not always possible due to certain post conditions that sometimes require officers to stay fixed for certain time periods, such as providing coverage of non-bulletproof booths. Such an assignment immobilizes the officer and encourages crime at other locations on a post. I must consider such conditions when I review why crimes occurred when an officer was assigned to a post.

I also require the sector sergeant to review officers' reports of their patrol activities during all tour hours. Review of all officers' activities is a must as a means of measuring both productivity and crime prevention effectiveness. Records are maintained depicting each officer's activity and a squad, platoon, anti-crime, and traffic control view of each member and the unit's productivity is available for immediate study. These records provide insight into each officer's performance and police activity.

It is more difficult to judge the officer's performance in providing other services such as aided cases, public relations and community relations. Looking strictly through statistical data does not necessarily capture an officer's effectiveness in these areas. So I make personal observations and solicit feedback from my subordinate superior officers. Also, the number of civilian complaints lodged against District 34 members is a good indicator of how some of the public perceive us.

Question: Are you utilizing a self-inspection system? If so, give details on what areas, how monitored, etc.

Answer: Self-inspection systems are being utilized in this command and vary according to the function such systems are designed to monitor. For example, take CRIME ANALYSIS. In order to cope with emerging crime conditions, it is necessary to continuously review all crime reports within the district. Aside from the "norm" of crime reports on required department forms such as TP-67s, TP-4s, TP-4E's, CCN #s, blotter entries, etc., District 34 crime analysis and statistics forms and procedures require:

1. Daily twenty-four hour recap of crimes.

2. Three-month felony comparison chart indicating when, where, how, and types of crime being committed.
3. Monthly felony and misdemeanor crime charts by rapid transit divisions.
4. A three-year bar chart showing felony and misdemeanor complaints and arrests.
5. A two-year pin chart depicting felony crime on all rapid transit lines in the command.
6. A four-year felony complaint chart maintained daily, coupled with the current month arrest charts.
7. Monthly crime statistics report.
8. Individual monthly activity charts of each officer's activity assigned to the command.
9. All District 34 activity logs.

All of the above information is maintained by one officer designated as the "crime analysis officer," who confers with me on a continual basis. Based on this information, manpower deployments are made or adjusted to emergency conditions. The crime information is given to the desk officers and patrol supervisors and is imparted to the patrol force through patrol assignments and roll call instructions.

Another area of self-inspection is PATROL PERFORMANCE, which is constantly checked by superior officers on patrol through patrol visits and observations of patrol members. Each superior officer has fixed responsibility for certain squads assigned to him. Additionally, all superior officers have administrative duties as outlined in our published guidelines entitled "Superior Officers' Duties & Responsibilities."

Personal observations are made by me of the various aspects of District 34's performance. These observations include foot patrol, train patrol, RMP patrol, desk officers, field supervisors, detectives, and the clerical staff. District 34 blotters and logs are also perused periodically by me.

Question: At present, what is your characterization of the state of your command and secondly, where do you perceive it will be one year from now?

Answer: My view of the general state of this command is one of an effective department unit, in spite of the continued increase in crime. Some of the factors that have contributed to that crime increase, a number of which are beyond the direct control of this command, include:

- 23% reduction in district manpower
- 75% reduction in Code 99 overtime
- Loss of city police coverage
- Changes in the socio-economic composition of area neighborhoods and schools

- Types of crime being committed by primarily young people
- Inability to obtain positive identification due to the speed with which many of the crimes are committed, and victims' fear of reprisal.
- Lack of reliable informants
- Crimes spread over wide areas

Despite the above, District 34 personnel will continue to make every effort to reduce crime and improve police services to the public and the Transit Authority. Morale is good, motivation positive with salaries and working conditions continuing to improve, and the pride of being a transit cop – all of which will continue to be factors that I believe will result in improved performance in the coming year.

Consistent with my earlier comment regarding demands from the community for transit police services, I was ordered to attend a meeting in the Brooklyn borough president's office one evening. Many neighborhood groups of civic-minded citizens were in attendance, making requests for more transit police coverage for their respective areas. I did my homework prior to the meeting and all the statistical data we collect and monitor was a great help in presenting the story to this group of very concerned citizens. The presentation emphasized that more than 70% of the transit crime was being committed by children less than eighteen years of age. Additionally, the crime statistics we reported supported how and where we deployed our resources.

Another concern of District 34 is the problem of crowd control due to the huge number of people who frequent the area, particularly during the spring and summer months. Historically, Easter Sunday sets the behavioral trend in the Coney Island area for the remainder of the spring, summer, and fall. Incidents and criminal activity on that particular day seems to attract troublemakers to the Coney Island area on subsequent weekends and holidays. Traditionally, both the transit and city police provide additional manpower to supplement local commands. This additional manpower is essential for maintaining orderly control of the crowds.

So far, both police departments have been able to maintain control of the holiday crowds at Coney Island, but we were not always so fortunate. Let me relate one incident that caused catastrophic results. On one of the major holiday weekends in the late '60s, close to a million people visited Coney Island and most of them used the transit system to get there. It had been a beautiful, clear day without a cloud in the sky. Suddenly, a tremendous rain storm developed, driving hundreds of thousands of people from the amusement area and from the beaches into the Stillwell Avenue station, all at once!

Now, there is no way to absorb that number of people in so short a period of time. Remember, each ten-car train can handle 2,000 passengers and with a "headway" of ten minutes between trains, that adds up to 12,000 passengers per hour for each of the five different lines leaving the area. Unfortunately, most of the people use the D line, so that one line was the cause of a complete bottleneck that bordered on riot-like conditions. The city police kept herding all the people off the beaches and into the subway station at Stillwell Avenue thinking it was a bottomless pit. Our guys were swamped with the mass of annoyed humanity leaping over turnstiles and trying to jamb themselves into overcrowded trains. Fights broke out, kids were screaming – things were really out of control. Reinforcements were sent in, entrances sealed off, people diverted to other stations or onto buses, and transit cops put on trains to try to keep order. Order finally was restored, but only after a bitter lesson was learned. Let's hope the brass never forgets.

Chapter 24

To give you a view of how the New York City newspapers felt the fight against subway crime was going, I have included excerpts from two articles.

Daily News
Thursday, April 9, 1981

Find city is stalled on crime train in losing subway war
By RICHARD ESPOSITO and RICHARD EDMONDS
A two-year "War on Subway Crime" that has cost the city $31.1 million in overtime has failed to reduce violence on the rapid transit system. In fact, crime increased 33.2% in the second year of the battle, compared with the first year's figures, the *Daily News* has found.

The findings come as the Economic Development Council yesterday announced a list of the major problems plaguing the city Transit Authority and offered to help recruit fellow executives to solve them.

The council, founded by Chase Manhattan Bank President David Rockefeller, proposed using a host of management techniques to help slow the breakdown of the city's bus and subway system.

Violent crime had appeared to be on a downward trend at the close of the first year after Mayor Koch's March 19, 1979 declaration of war against subway felons. There were 10,726 reported felonies, compared with 1978, when the grim figure stood at 14,125. But the number quickly increased in the warmer months of 1980, and by the end of the second year of the crime war, felonies exceeded those for the calendar year 1978. For example, crime increased 74.3% in June 1980 over the same month in 1979.

From April 1980 through March 1981, there were 14,296 reported murders, rapes, assaults, thefts, burglaries, and larcenies, according to figures obtained from the TA Police Department. In the last two years, cops served 2,370 eight-hour overtime tours. The TA now has 2,138 officers on patrol throughout the 230 mile system, and 177 rookies are in training at the Police Academy. When the war started, there were 2,441 officers.

Deputy Chief John Rogan says the crime increase can be traced to "jewelry-related" incidents, such as necklace snatches. But his frustration, he says, "stems from an inadequate criminal justice system that produces repeat offenders."

New York Post
Friday, August 1, 1980

The Subways Aren't For Sleeping As Crime Soars
By Philip Messing

Drastic cutbacks in Transit Authority manpower on Coney Island trains have led to a startling 500% increase in "lush working" crimes committed against sleeping or unaware subway passengers, *The Post* has learned.

"It has become physically impossible to keep up with the number of sneak thieves who are victimizing unsuspecting passengers late at night," said Det. Joseph Edwards, assigned to District 34 Investigations at Coney Island's Stillwell Av. Station. Police described "lush working" as a "crime of opportunity" where wily criminals spot tipsy or tired subway riders late at night, wait until they fall asleep and then slash at their pockets or purses with razors as the train pulls into deserted terminals. "They have hands as steady as surgeons," said Det. Edwards. "You don't know they've hit until you leave the train without your wallet." Many of the victims are people returning home exhausted from work, he said. District 34 sources say in the calendar year ending December 1979 — when 12 men were assigned to lush working detail — 48 people were victimized. But since January of this year — with the Stillwell Av. Lush working detail cut from 12 men to 8, and finally just a two-man team working several times a week — there have been 132 lush working complaints. There have been 18 arrests this year, with 12 coming in the past 2 ½ months, police said. "It used to be that we could keep them out by running into the same faces," said TA cop George Adinolfi, a TPBA delegate who sometimes works during the prime lush working hours of 12 a.m. to 5 a.m. "But they're not getting caught as frequently so I guess more of them are coming out of the woodwork." District 34 manpower declined from 147 men to 86 in the last 2 ½ years. Cops say the most dangerous trains to ride late at night when you're less than fully awake are the F, D and RR lines. Stillwell Av. TA cops also police the B, N and QB lines. Subway passengers can avoid being the victim of a lush worker by not falling asleep on the subways and riding with the conductor.

Naturally, when the above-cited article was read by the brass downtown, I received a call inquiring into the validity of their statements. The part about the reduction in manpower was certainly true, but the number of increased lush working complaints was nowhere near the inflated figure quoted. I had assigned a two-man team to "late tours" and those two guys had made a terrific amount of lush worker collars, which showed we were on top of the problem. Unfortunately, Stillwell Avenue, being a terminal and last stop, was where this type of crime was reported, and so District 34 got stuck with the complaint being charged to us – even though the victim may have boarded the train in the Bronx, fallen asleep immediately, and somewhere only God and the perpetrator knew between the Bronx and Coney Island, the crime was committed. Try to solve that one! So, what we do is make plainclothes assignments and make collars. Most of those arrested lived in other parts of the city, so you know that they hit their victims where and when the opportunity presented itself, and not necessarily in Coney Island!

The war on crime, like life, goes on and on, with no easy or quick solutions. Just day-to-day battles, good guys against bad guys, with the public right in the middle of it.

One more final article that appeared in the *New York Times* on Sunday, January 25, 1981 provided an update on what has been done with the mayor's plan to "merge" the three police departments into one force. In that article, it was reported that Mayor Koch found that it would be too costly to proceed with the merger of the city's three police forces. Apparently, after studying the situation for some eighteen months, there were just too many economic and political hurdles to overcome to make it feasible. The study indicated that about $30 million would be required to integrate the three communications systems. Nevertheless, the city plans on revisiting the idea sometime in the future.

So there you have it, no consolidation <u>again</u> as I predicted earlier in my story! At least this time they sunk it with dignity. There is a great deal of truth to the report, but we now have in fact, de facto consolidation since the three forces are informally under the final control of the city police commissioner. And we do have improved coordination at the very top. We do not have any noticeable improved coordination at the gut level of execution – in the trenches – between the field forces. We still have our daily skirmishes relative to on-going field problems. "That's in the subway or on the bus – it's theirs, not ours." Or from us, "That's the streets – they've got it." In reality, wherever it happens in the city, it's both our problem. Until we accept that concept, neither of us has really learned anything. The public belongs to us and WE have to protect them – WHEREVER!

I would like to offer one final comment on it costing $30 million to convert the three communication systems. Maybe so, but instant communication is available simply by exchanging some portable radios among the three departments, exchanging some radio cars, and installing some additional telephones – and that doesn't cost $30 million!

Still, life goes on in the Big Apple. People continue to get killed every day as they do in lots of places. It's not the mayor's fault, or the fault of the police, or even the town itself. It's society's fault and we better find some answers soon, so our kids, and their kids, can believe in and be proud of America. Over the past three years, twenty-three police officers from the three police forces have been killed. The most recent one involved John "Jerry" Scarangella of the 113th Precinct, who was struck down in a hail of 9-mm bullets. His partner was hit eleven times and survived. Officer Scarangella's younger brother, Luke, is a transit cop and works with me. I had to give him the word the day his brother was shot. That was tough, very tough. Recently,

George Steinbrenner, owner of the Yankees, had Luke and his brother's family to a Yankee game where he presented a $10,000 check to each of Jerry Scarangella's four children. What a wonderful thing to do!

Chapter 25

Not much more to my story now, except to add that we bought a house in Palm Coast, Florida, a beautiful community on the northeast coast, about twenty-three miles south of St. Augustine. It has championship golf courses, a marina and yacht club, and all very affordable. We are looking forward to retirement, once I finally decide "to pull the pin." I am thinking that the end of this year will be just about right. Retirement comes to many of us someday, and those of us in police service are fortunate to have the opportunity to retire at a comparatively young age, with excellent pension benefits. Lately, I think more and more about packing it in, thinking about days off, playing golf, and escaping the snow and ice of winter. So I know within myself that the time is getting closer for this old happy warrior to retire.

I feel a bit like General Custer might have felt at the "Little Big Horn" – I look around and only about twelve guys are still on the job from our 1950 class of recruits. All the others are gone. Some left for other jobs; some passed away; and the rest have all retired. Many of the retired ones have moved to the "Sun Belt" where the weather is warm and sunny most of the time, and where there are no subways! From a financial standpoint, it sure doesn't make much sense for the twelve of us to keep working – we don't make that much more than we'd be getting from our pensions. Nobody lives forever and I'd like to enjoy whatever years the Good Lord grants me. He has granted me good health and I intend to spend my retirement with my best gal, Eileen – trying to improve our golf games, enjoying some travel, enjoying the company of some good friends, and seeing as much as possible our two fine children and our five beautiful grandchildren. I look forward to seeing more of my many relatives, and maybe even joining a country club – if I can find one reasonably priced – and just enjoying the good life. I know somehow that it really can't be better than the life I have known. The Lord has been so good to me through these fifty-six years. How else can you account for all the good things that have happened to me?

The final stages of this book would not be complete if I did not mention one of the great pleasures – and a most distinct honor – I have had afforded me these past three years. I was given the honor of leading our Emerald Society Members up "The Avenue" on Saint Patrick's Day. This past March 17th, my entire family, including the grandchildren, was there to see "Pop-Pop" in his captain's uniform, followed by "The Pipers" and all those other grand, smiling police officers. It was a proud moment on such a grand occasion – one that I, and my family, will never forget! Someone took pictures of me leading the parade as Marshal, and a picture of me returning to the line of march after stopping off to kiss the cardinal's ring on the steps of St. Patrick's. Don't be fooled by the angelic look! I hung both of these pictures in our dining room for all to see.

When I finally "pull the pin" and leave police service, I will leave with a good feeling because I have loved almost every minute of it. The job has been good to me in so many ways. It provided the means to raise and educate my family, buy a house, afford vacation trips and all the necessities of life, plus enable us to enjoy a few luxuries. I will leave police service knowing that three of my nephews are police officers, plus another nephew is a corrections officer. I am certain that they will improve on their uncle's record!

This book is but a feeble attempt to characterize the splendid work of the members of the Transit Police Department. The magnitude of their daily efforts to protect the riding public could never be adequately conveyed in one book, particularly by a writer as inept as this one! I hope that the book at least gives you some insight into the job that our members do, and what they are up against from their very first day on the job. I have only written about situations that I was personally involved in, or knew about as a result of my being a commanding officer of various districts.

Thank you for taking the time to read my book, and if you're ever on the golf course and see a white-haired guy hitting a wicked slice off the tee, look out – it may be me!

I'm ending my story with a copy of "The Police Officer's

Prayer to Saint Michael," considered the patron saint of all policemen. Again, thanks for listening.

THE POLICE OFFICER'S PRAYER TO ST. MICHAEL

Saint Michael, heaven's glorious commissioner of police, who once so neatly and successfully cleared God's premises of all its undesirables, look with kindly and professional eyes on your earthly force.

Give us cool heads, stout hearts, and uncanny flair for investigation and wise judgment.

Make us the terror of burglars, the friend of children and law-abiding citizens, kind to strangers, polite to bores, strict with law-breakers and impervious to temptations.

You know, Saint Michael, from your own experiences with the devil that the police officer's lot on earth is not always a happy one; but your sense of duty that so pleased God, your hard knocks that so surprised the devil, and your angelic self-control give us inspiration.

And when we lay down our night sticks, enroll us in your heavenly force, where we will be as proud to guard the throne of God as we have been to guard the city of all the people. Amen.

The Final Chapter

My dad died of a heart attack on Friday, March 27th, 1998. He was hitting balls near his home in Palm Coast, Florida – not on the golf course, but rather, at a spot over by the Intracoastal Waterway. He was always an early riser and that morning, after enjoying a few cups of coffee, he headed out to hit a few. And just like that, the "Man Upstairs" called him home. His obituary was published the following Wednesday in *Newsday*. Tom O'Rourke, the very first chief of the Transit Police, said "John did a great deal of good for a tremendous number of people in law enforcement. He was intuitively a leader. A man of integrity, a man of intelligence. He was one of the finest men I've ever known."

Some time after Dad passed away, I got hold of the binder that contained Dad's story. My sister had it in her possession and I asked if she would mind my borrowing it for a while. I intended to jump right into it. But I let life get in the way and put it off, burying the binder in a storage box in my basement. One day recently, I was down in the basement looking for something when I opened the box with the binder. I grabbed hold of it and haven't put it down since. I decided not just to read it, but to make sure others would have the opportunity to read it as well. I began the task of converting the typewritten pages in his binder into an electronic document for publication.

I was on a mission and my dad, as was his custom, made things pretty easy for me. He was always a wonderful storyteller and as I read and edited here and there, I wanted to make sure that his story, and the many stories he had to tell, came through loud and clear.

My dad was so loved – by his family, his friends, and the many police officers who worked with him. In Dad's best storytelling tradition, I want to tell a little story. My dad's passing was so sudden, we were all left a bit shell-shocked. My oldest daughter, Denise, was living in Alexandria, Virginia at the time, where she was teaching. My son, Brian, was at Penn State. My daughter, Karolyn, was at the University of Delaware. My sister's two kids, Aimee and Robbie, were also both pretty far away – Robbie at Radford College in Virginia and Aimee, living and working in Atlanta. We had no choice but to deliver the news by telephone. That was tough, certainly for them as well as for us. Thankfully, they each had the support of their friends. As they each made the necessary arrangements to get home, I focused on my mom.

My dad's brother Bob and his wife Ellen were visiting my parents when my dad passed. I wanted to jump on a plane and fly down to be with my mom, but Uncle Bob and Aunt Ellen insisted they had Florida covered. I made sure Mom was OK and stayed in communication with her all weekend – something I am not at all good at. I focused my energy on getting the arrangements in place on this end, for Mom decided to have the funeral services on Long Island, which was clearly the right choice. I wanted to celebrate Dad's life – he deserved that, having done so much, for so many. I started reaching out to the PBA, friends from the job, the newspapers, the Emerald Society, and on and on.

Since my dad retired in 1982, I wasn't sure how many people would remember him. The funeral mass was held at Holy Name of Jesus Church in Woodbury and my parents' good friend, Monsignor Jolley, presided. When we arrived at the funeral home in Plainview to say a final goodbye to Dad before heading over to the church, a couple of Nassau County motorcycle cops and patrol cars from the Nassau County and Suffolk County Police Departments were on hand to provide an escort. When we arrived at the church, there must have been twenty-five bagpipers lined up. And after the service, police units escorted us all the way to the city line where they handed us off to the NYPD. The NYPD actually closed down our side of the Throgs Neck Bridge in honor of my dad as the funeral procession headed to Dad's final resting place at Gate of Heaven Cemetery in Valhalla, New York. New York state troopers met us for the final few miles to the cemetery. I was so proud, and I am sure my dad was there in spirit, standing tall and snapping a crisp salute to his fellow officers. Many had remembered Dad, and their tribute helped to ease the pain for all of us.

My dad truly was a born leader, a person who did what he said he was going to do, and a person who was willing to make personal sacrifices to make sure it happened. He had the unique ability to motivate the people who worked for him in such a positive way that they would jump through hoops to get the job done, just looking forward to seeing that wonderful smile on my dad's face and receiving his heartfelt pat on their backs. I found in my own career how truly unique that capability is. And it seems that other managers who don't have that innate ability resent those that do. They rationalize that people will take advantage of that kind of management style – that being too "soft" leads to poor performance and ineffectiveness. My personal experience says quite the opposite.

Clearly, my dad did not agree with his superiors who seemed to feel that "once a union guy, always a union guy." They missed the point. As Dad states in his book, patrol officers are the ones who truly provide the police services to the public. Give them what they need to get the job done, listen to their ideas for improving how things get done, and then go get them the things they need and reward them whenever you can – it never grows old. But it has to be genuine, not patronizing. We knew the difference when we were all kids, and we still know the difference now! Simple when you think about it, and no one was better at it than my dad.

Dad truly was an innovative thinker. As you can tell from his story, he was always thinking "out of the box" to come up with better ways of operating. Why did guys patrolling our subways need patrol cars and scooters? Well, he knew and he pushed hard to get them, knowing that equipment like that would make a real difference. For such an innovative guy and intuitive leader, he didn't "shoot from the hip" – he relied on a lot of data and observation to guide his decisions. He just never let the numbers tell the whole story. He knew people, often making split-second decisions under incredible pressure, were the ones to get it done.

At Dad's testimonial dinner, which was so well attended by the rank and file – kind of unique for a superior officer – I sat next to his old partner, Jim Rooney. Jim said, "You know, Brian, if your dad had never been PBA president, he would have been chief of detectives today."

I looked around the room and then replied, "Jim, just look at this place. All of these people here to honor him for all that he has done for the job, and for them. I don't think you could do it any better. Your right, he should have been rewarded for his tremendous leadership. But in the end, this is what really matters – way more than being a chief."

Dad was truly my hero, and always will be. There is never a time I don't think about how he would have handled things. And even though I fail quite often, I try to emulate many of his wonderful qualities. Finding his manuscript again and getting so deeply into this book has been a wonderful experience. It has been twelve years since my dad passed, but having the chance to relive all the moments he describes in the book has kind of renewed our relationship. I laughed, I shed a tear or two, and I got angry when I felt his disappointment. But in the end, I felt the same way I did at his testimonial dinner over thirty years ago … he really got it right.

My mom and dad had been married a month shy of fifty-one years when he passed away. She never really adjusted to life without him. She had many friends and a wonderful relationship with many of my dad's brothers and sisters. She would spend about five months in Palm Coast and then head north for the remainder of the year. She would use our house as her base of operations, but would spend a lot of time with my Uncle Buddy and Aunt Barbara at their home in Wantagh. Buddy was Dad's youngest brother, and Buddy and Barbara always took such wonderful care of my mom, particularly after Dad had left us. I know he is very thankful for their love and support. In August 2002, while spending a few days up in the "Irish Catskills" with friends and family, my mom suffered a brain aneurysm. She underwent four hours of surgery up in Albany, New York. Initially, things looked promising. But in the end, she kind of slipped into a rough place. She lasted about a year, passing away on August 3rd, 2003. I think she just wanted to be with my dad again.

My dad was not here for the September 11th, 2001 attacks. I have often wondered how he would have reacted and I felt that maybe it was better he wasn't here to see it. But then I realized – here was a guy who survived the longest surface battle in naval history during World War II at the Battle of the Komandorski Islands, who served for thirty-three years as a police officer in New York City, and who helped to raise a bunch of younger brother and sisters on the streets of New York – he would have handled it. And he would have been very proud of his fellow police officers and firefighters in how they responded. He clearly would have been dismayed by the human condition, and the bad things we seem to continue to do to one another. But he had seen evil manifest itself many times and when things seem bleakest, someone -- or lots of ones -- step up and make a difference. People did step up that day and he would have been very proud of them.

My dad loved his grandchildren so much and he was proud of each of them. Robbie and Brian played hockey and soccer together in high school and he loved to see them play. Karolyn played field hockey in high school and even though I am not sure he understood all the rules, he was thrilled to see her play. Aimee and Denise both danced and he spent lots of hours at recitals cheering them on. I am sure he is very proud of the men and women they have become – he served as such a wonderful role model for them.

My sister, Susan was always the apple of Dad's eye. She has a lot of Dad's drive in her and much of his fashion sense.

He always looked sharp, and so does she. My wife, Kathy, had always been another daughter to him. He loved her for being the special person she is, and for putting up with his son for all these years. I have my mother-in-law Margaret and father-in-law Tom to thank for giving me such a wonderful partner and friend.

My dad is the great-grandfather to six beautiful children – Christian and Reilly (children of my daughter Denise and son-in law Chris); Jackson and Sophia (children of my son Brian and daughter-in-law Christina); Michael (child of my daughter Karolyn and son-in-law Mike); and Andrew (child of my nephew Rob Kemp and his wife Kasey). Everyone loved my dad and kids were especially fond of him. He knew how to make everyone feel good about themselves, and that included the little people. He made time to talk to everyone and the kids loved to play with him. I regret his great-grandchildren didn't get to meet him, but I can't help but notice many of his fine qualities in them – and that gives me a great sense of peace.

In closing, I want to thank you for taking the time to read my dad's book. Any errors in converting Dad's manuscript are my fault, not his. Dad would have listed the many friends, family, and fellow cops in the book and probably written something about each of them. I chose to keep it "short and sweet" and hopefully, will not have offended anyone by doing so. I have included some photographs in the book as a personal touch. Through those photos, you will meet some of Dad's family and friends.

Thank you again for reading my dad's book. I hope you enjoyed it as much as I enjoyed helping to bring it to you.

Brian R. Martin
The Author's Son
September 15, 2010

Photographic Memorabilia

My Dad as a Navy Quartermaster

My Dad as a Detective

Mom and Dad on Their Wedding Day

Dada Pete and Gert, my Dad's Stepfather and Mother

My Dad and His Brother Tommy

My Dad's Big Brother, Matthew, Known as Pep

My Dad and his Lifelong Friend, Lou Smellings

My Dad's Sister Vivian and Her Husband, Syd Bunting

My Mom's Brother and Dad's Friend, Jack Keena

The Transit Police Department Patch

My Dad in His Garage in Palm Coast, Proudly Displaying
His Police Rank Atop a U.S.S. Bailey Anchor

My Dad's Mom, Gert with Corsage and My Dad's Sisters,
Bernadette, Adrian (Tippy) and Jean

Deck: Brother-in-Law Ken (Tippy's husband), Russell (Buddy),
　　　　Donald (Butchie)
1st Step: Barbara (Buddy's Wife), Jean
2nd Step: Tippy, Ann (Pep's Wife)
Top Step: Audrey (Butchie's Wife), Dorothy, Dad, Mom, Dick
　　　　(Jean's Husband)

Dad, Mom, Susan and Me Back in 1955

My Dad and Me in 1955

My Dad and Me Some Thirty Years Later, After He Retired

My Dad's Last Christmas With His Family, December 25, 1997
Front Row: Dad and His Grandsons, Robbie and Brian
Back Row: Susan, Mom, Karolyn, Denise, Aimee, Kathy,
Our Dog Bailey, Me

A Proud Moment for Dad, Leading His Fellow Officers
up Fifth Avenue on St. Patrick's Day

Dad with That Angelic Look After Having Greeted
the Cardinal at St. Patrick's Cathedral

At my Dad's Testimonial Dinner After Having served as
Transit PBA President and New York State PBA President
Left to Right: Ellen (My Dad's Sister-in-law and Bob's Wife),
Dad, Mom, John Nove and His Wife, Marie
and Steve O'Connor, Ginny and Frank Begley,
My Dad's Brother Bob

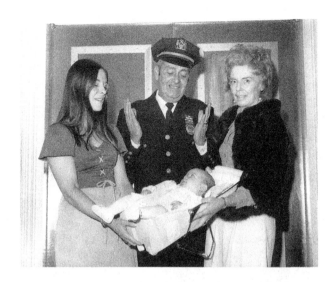

A Proud Day for My Dad – the Day He Made Captain
He Is with Susan, His First Grandchild, Aimee, and My Mom

My Dad Sitting at His Desk in One of His Commands –
He Had Three: District 11, District 3, and District 34.
As you can see, he used a lot of data to support his deci-
sions and the innovative thinking he brought to the job.

My Dad at His Retirement Dinner

★ ★ ★ ★ ★ ★ ★ ★ ★ ★
SERVED ON
U.S.S. **BAILEY**
DD-492
1942-1946

ALEUTIANS • TARAWA • KWAJALEIN • BORNEO • OKINAWA
SAIPAN • TINIAN • PELELIU • PHILIPPINES

My Dad's ID card signifying his service on the U.S.S. Bailey,
the flagship of the 14th Destroyer Squadron of the Pacific
Fleet, and participant in the longest surface battle
in naval history - the Battle of the Komandorski Islands,
March 26, 1943

CPSIA information can be obtained
at www.ICGtesting.com
Printed in the USA
BVOW06s1915160317
478389BV00023B/40/P

9 781432 765897